# Prayers That Avail Much

## Volume I

### James 5:16

*by*
*Word Ministries, Inc.*

And this is the confidence that we have in him, that, if we ask any thing according to his will, he heareth us: and if we know that he hear us, whatsoever we ask, we know that we have the petitions that we desired of him.

1 John 5:14,15

**Harrison House**
Tulsa, Oklahoma

*20th Printing*
*Over 730,000 in print.*

*Prayers That Avail Much — Volume I*
ISBN 0-89274-590-8
Copyright © 1989 by Word Ministries, Inc.
P. O. Box 76532
Atlanta, Georgia 30358

Published by Harrison House, Inc.
P. O. Box 35035
Tulsa, Oklahoma 74153

# DEDICATION

This book is dedicated to our Lord and Savior Jesus Christ.

**The Lord gave the Word: great was the company of those that published it.**

**Psalm 68:11**

Special thanks to Jan Duncan, Carolyn East, Pat Gastineau, Frankie Patterson, Barbara Patton, and Pat Porter for their share in this book.

Germaine Copeland, President
Word Ministries, Inc.

# CONTENTS

## II. Intercessory Prayers for Others

### Prayers for God's People and Ministries

### Prayers for the World

Prayers for Those in Authority

Prayers for the Needs of Others

# FOREWORD

The prayers in this book are to be used by you for yourself and for others. They are a matter of the heart. Deliberately feed them into your spirit. Allow the Holy Spirit to make the Word a reality in your heart. Your spirit will become quickened to God's Word, and you will begin to think like God thinks and talk like He talks. You will find yourself poring over His Word — hungering for more and more. The Father rewards those who diligently seek Him. (Heb. 11:6.)

Meditate upon the Scriptures listed with these prayers. These are by no means the only Scriptures on certain subjects, but they are a beginning.

These prayers are to be a help and a guide to you in order for you to get better acquainted with your heavenly Father and His Word. Not only does His Word affect your life, but also it will affect others through you, for you will be able to counsel accurately those who come to you for advice. If you cannot counsel someone with the Word, you do not have anything with which to counsel. Walk in God's counsel, and prize His wisdom. (Ps. 1; Prov. 4:7,8.) People are looking for something on which they can depend. When someone in need comes to you, you can point him to that portion in God's Word that is the answer to his problem. You become victorious, trustworthy, and the one with the answer, for your heart is fixed and established on His Word. (Ps. 112.)

Once you begin delving into God's Word, you must commit to ordering your conversation aright. (Ps. 50:23.) That is being a doer of the Word. Faith always has a good report. You cannot pray effectively for yourself, for someone else, or about something and then talk negatively about the matter. (Matt. 12:34-37.) This is being double-minded, and a double-minded man receives *nothing* from God. (James 1:6-8.)

In Ephesians 4:29,30 AMP it is written:

> Let no foul or polluting language, nor evil word, nor unwholesome or worthless talk [ever] come out of your mouth; but only such [speech] as is good and beneficial to the spiritual progress of others, as is fitting to the need and the occasion, that it may be a blessing and give grace (God's favor) to those who hear it.

> And do not grieve the Holy Spirit of God, (do not offend, or vex, or sadden Him) by whom you were sealed (marked, branded as God's own, secured) for the day of redemption — of final deliverance through Christ from evil and the consequences of sin.

Allow these words to sink into your innermost being. Our Father has much, so very much, to say about that little member, the tongue. (James 3.) Give the devil no opportunity by getting into worry, unforgiveness, strife, and criticism. Put a stop to idle and foolish talking. (Eph. 4:27; 5:4.) You are to be a blessing to others. (Gal. 6:10.)

*Talk the answer, not the problem. The answer is in God's Word.* You must have knowledge of that Word — revelation knowledge. (1 Cor. 2:7-16.)

As an intercessor, unite with others in prayer. United prayer is a mighty weapon that the Body of Christ is to use.

Believe you receive when you pray. Confess the Word. Hold fast to your confession of faith in God's Word. Allow your spirit to pray by the Holy Spirit. Praise God for the victory *now* before any manifestation. *Walk by faith and not by sight.* (2 Cor. 5:7.)

Don't be moved by adverse circumstances. As Satan attempts to challenge you, resist him steadfast in the faith — letting patience have her perfect work. (James 1:4.) Take the Sword of the Spirit and the shield of faith and quench his every fiery dart. (Eph. 6:16,17.) The entire substitutionary work of Christ was for you. Satan is now a defeated foe because Jesus conquered him. (Col. 2:14,15.) Satan is overcome by the blood of the Lamb and the Word of our testimony. (Rev. 12:11.) Fight the good fight of faith. (1 Tim. 6:12.) Withstand the adversary and be firm in faith against his onset — rooted, established, strong, and determined. (1 Pet. 5:9.) Speak God's Word boldly and courageously.

Your desire should be to please and to bless the Father. As you pray in line with His Word, He joyfully hears that you — His child — are living and walking in the Truth. (3 John 4.)

How exciting to know that the prayers of the saints are forever in the throne room. (Rev. 5:8.) Hallelujah!

Praise God for His Word and the limitlessness of prayer in the name of Jesus. It belongs to every child of God. Therefore, run with patience the race that is set before you, looking unto Jesus the author and finisher of your faith. (Heb. 12:1,2.) God's Word is able to build you up and give you your rightful inheritance among all God's set apart ones. (Acts 20:32.)

*Commit yourself to pray and to pray correctly by approaching the throne with your mouth filled with His Word!*

# INTRODUCTION

...The earnest (heart-felt, continued) prayer of
a righteous man makes tremendous power available
— dynamic in its working.

James 5:16 AMP

Prayer is fellowshiping with the Father — a vital, personal contact with God Who is more than enough. We are to be in constant communion with Him:

For the eyes of the Lord are upon the righteous
— those who are upright and in right standing with
God — and His ears are attentive (open) to their
prayer....

1 Peter 3:12 AMP

Prayer is not to be a religious form with no power. It is to be effective and accurate and bring *results*. God watches over His Word to perform it. (Jer. 1:12.)

Prayer that brings results must be based on God's Word.

For the Word that God speaks is alive and full of
power — making it active, operative, energizing and
effective; it is sharper than any two-edged sword,
penetrating to the dividing line of the breath of life
(soul) and [the immortal] spirit, and of joints and
marrow [that is, of the deepest parts of our nature]
exposing and sifting and analyzing and judging the
very thoughts and purposes of the heart.

Hebrews 4:12 AMP

Prayer is this "living" Word in our mouths. Our mouths must speak forth faith, for faith is what pleases God. (Heb. 11:6.) We hold His Word up to Him in prayer, and our Father sees Himself in His Word.

God's Word is our contact with Him. We put Him in remembrance of His Word (Is. 43:26) placing a demand on His ability in the name of our Lord Jesus. We remind Him that He supplies all of our needs according to His riches in glory by Christ Jesus. (Phil. 4:19.) That Word does not return to Him void — without producing any effect, useless — but it *shall* accomplish that which He pleases and purposes, and it shall prosper in the thing for which He sent it. (Is. 55:11.) Hallelujah!

God did *not* leave us without His thoughts and His ways for we have His Word — His bond. God instructs us to call Him, and He will answer and show us great and mighty things. (Jer. 33:3.) Prayer is to be exciting — not drudgery.

It takes someone to pray. God moves as we pray in faith — believing. He says that His eyes run to and fro throughout the whole earth to show Himself strong in behalf of those whose hearts are blameless toward Him. (2 Chron. 16:9.) We are blameless. (Eph. 1:4.) We are His very own children. (Eph. 1:5.) We are His righteousness in Christ Jesus. (2 Cor. 5:21.) He tells us to come boldly to the throne of grace and *obtain* mercy and find grace to help in time of need — appropriate and well-timed help. (Heb. 4:16.) Praise the Lord!

The prayer armor is for every believer, every member of the Body of Christ, who will put it on and walk in it, for the weapons of our warfare are *not carnal* but mighty through God for the pulling down of the strongholds of the enemy (Satan, the god of this world, and all his demonic forces). Spiritual warfare takes place in prayer. (2 Cor. 10:4, Eph. 6:12,18.)

There are many different kinds of prayer, such as the prayer of thanksgiving and praise, the prayer of dedication and worship, and the prayer that changes *things* (not God). All prayer involves a time of fellowshiping with the Father.

In Ephesians 6, we are instructed to take the Sword of the Spirit which is the Word of God and **pray at all times — on every occasion, in every season — in the Spirit, with all [manner of] prayer and entreaty** (Eph. 6:18 AMP).

In 1 Timothy 2 we are admonished and urged that **petitions, prayers, intercessions and thanksgivings be offered on behalf of all men** (1 Tim. 2:1 AMP). *Prayer is our responsibility.*

Prayer must be the foundation of every Christian endeavor. Any failure is a prayer failure. We are *not* to be ignorant concerning God's Word. God desires for His people to be successful, to be filled with a full, deep, and clear knowledge of His will (His Word), and to bear fruit in every good work. (Col. 1:9-13.) We then bring honor and glory to Him. (John 15:8.) He desires that we know how to pray for **the prayer of the upright is his delight** (Prov. 15:8).

Our Father has not left us helpless. Not only has He given us His Word, but also He has given us the Holy Spirit to help our infirmities when we know not how to pray as we ought. (Rom. 8:26.) Praise God! Our Father has provided His people with every possible avenue to insure their complete and total victory in this life in the name of our Lord Jesus. (1 John 5:3-5.)

*We pray to the Father, in the name of Jesus, through the Holy Spirit, according to the Word!*

Using God's Word on purpose, specifically, in prayer is one means of prayer, and it is a most effective and accurate means. Jesus said, **The words (truths) that I have been speaking to you are spirit and life** (John 6:63 AMP).

When Jesus faced Satan in the wilderness, He said, "It is written. . .it is written. . .it is written." We are to live, be upheld, and sustained by every Word that proceeds from the mouth of God. (Matt. 4:4.)

James, by the Spirit, admonishes that we do not have, because we do not ask. We ask and receive not, because we ask amiss. (James 4:2,3.) We must heed that admonishment now for we are to become experts in prayer rightly dividing the Word of Truth. (2 Tim. 2:15.)

Using the Word in prayer is *not* taking it out of context, for His Word in us is the key to answered prayer — to prayer that brings results. He is able to do exceedingly abundantly above all we ask or think, according to the power that works in us. (Eph. 3:20.) The power lies within God's Word. It is anointed by the Holy Spirit. The Spirit of God does not lead us apart from the Word, for the Word is of the Spirit of God. We apply that Word personally to ourselves and to others — not adding to or taking from it — in the name of Jesus. We apply the Word to the *now* — to those things, circumstances, and situations facing each of us *now*.

Paul was very specific and definite in his praying. The first chapters of Ephesians, Philippians, Colossians, and 2 Thessalonians are examples of how Paul prayed for believers. There are numerous others. *Search them out.* Paul wrote under the inspiration of the Holy Spirit. We can use these Spirit-given prayers today!

In 2 Corinthians 1:11, 2 Corinthians 9:14, and Philippians 1:4, we see examples of how believers prayed one for another — putting others first in their prayer life with *joy.* Our faith does work by love. (Gal. 5:6.) We grow spiritually as we reach out to help others — praying for and with them and holding out to them the Word of Life. (Phil. 2:16.)

Man is a spirit, he has a soul, and he lives in a body. (1 Thess. 5:23.) In order to operate successfully, each of these three parts must be fed properly. The soul or intellect feeds on intellectual food to produce intellectual strength. The body feeds on physical food to produce physical strength. The spirit — the heart or inward man — is the real you, the part that has been reborn in Christ Jesus. It must feed on spirit food which is God's Word in order to produce and develop faith. As we feast upon God's Word, our minds become renewed with His Word, and we have a fresh mental and spiritual attitude. (Eph. 4:23,24.)

Likewise, we are to present our bodies a living sacrifice, holy, acceptable unto God (Rom. 12:1) and not let that body dominate us but bring it into subjection to the spirit man. (1 Cor. 9:27.) God's Word is healing and health to all our flesh. (Prov. 4:22.) Therefore, God's Word affects each part of us — spirit, soul and body. We become vitally united to the Father, to Jesus, and to the Holy Spirit — one with Them. (John 16:13-15, John 17:21, Col. 2:10.)

God's Word, this spirit food, takes root in our hearts, is formed by the tongue, and is spoken out of our mouths. This is creative power. The spoken Word works as we confess it and then apply the action to it.

Be doers of the Word, and not hearers only, deceiving your own selves. (James 1:22.) Faith without works or corresponding action is *dead*. (James 2:17.) Don't be mental assenters — those who agree that the Bible is true but never act on it. *Real faith is acting on God's Word now.* We cannot build faith without practicing the Word. We cannot develop an effective prayer life that is anything but empty words unless God's Word actually has a part in our lives. We are to hold fast to our *confession* of the Word's truthfulness. Our Lord Jesus is the High Priest of our confession (Heb. 3:1), and He is the Guarantee of a better agreement — a more excellent and advantageous covenant. (Heb. 7:22.)

*Prayer does not cause faith to work, but faith causes prayer to work.* Therefore, any prayer problem is a problem of doubt — doubting the integrity of the Word and the ability of God to stand behind His promises or the statements of fact in the Word.

We can spend fruitless hours in prayer if our hearts are not prepared beforehand. Preparation of the heart, the spirit, comes from meditation in the Father's Word, meditation on who we are in Christ, what He is to us, and what the Holy Spirit can mean to us as we become God-inside minded. As God told Joshua (Josh. 1:8), as we meditate on the Word day and night, and do according to all that is written, then shall we make our way prosperous and have good success. We are to attend to God's Word, submit to His sayings, keep them in the center of our hearts, and put away contrary talk. (Prov. 4:20-24.)

When we use God's Word in prayer, this is *not* something we just rush through uttering once, and we are finished. Do *not* be mistaken. There is nothing "magical" nor "manipulative" about it — no set pattern or device in order to satisfy what we want or think out of our flesh. Instead we are holding God's Word before Him. We confess what He says belongs to us.

*We expect His divine intervention while we choose not to look at the things that are seen but at the things that are unseen, for the things that are seen are subject to change.* (2 Cor. 4:18.)

Prayer based upon the Word rises above the senses, contacts the Author of the Word and sets His spiritual laws into motion. It is not just saying prayers that gets results, but it is spending time with the Father, learning His wisdom, drawing on His strength, being filled with His quietness, and basking in His love that bring results to our prayers. Praise the Lord!

\*　　\*　　\*

The prayers in this book are designed to teach and train you in the art of personal confession and intercessory prayer. As you pray them, you will be reinforcing the prayer armor which we have been instructed to put on in Ephesians 6:11. The fabric from which the armor is made is the Word of God. We are to live by every word that proceeds from the mouth of God. We desire the whole counsel of God, because we know it changes us. By receiving that counsel, you will be ... **transformed (changed) by the [entire] renewal of your mind — by its new ideals and attitude — so that you may prove [for yourselves] what is the good and acceptable and perfect will of God, even the thing which is good and acceptable and perfect [in His sight for you]** (Rom. 12:2 AMP).

The prayers of personal confession of the Word of God for yourself can also be used as intercessory prayers for others by simply praying them in the third person, changing the pronouns *I* or *we* to the name of the person or persons for whom you are interceding and adjusting the verbs accordingly.

The prayers of intercession have blanks in which you (individually or as a group) are to fill in the spaces with the name of the person(s) for whom you are praying. These prayers of intercession can likewise be made into prayers of personal confession for yourself (or your group) by inserting your own name(s) and the proper personal pronouns in the appropriate places.

An often-asked question is: "How many times should I pray the same prayer?"

The answer is simple: you pray until you know that the answer is fixed in your heart. After that, you need to repeat the prayer whenever adverse circumstances or long delays cause you to be tempted to doubt that your prayer has been heard and your request granted.

The Word of God is your weapon against the temptation to lose heart and grow weary in your prayer life. When that Word of promise becomes fixed in your heart, you will find yourself praising, giving glory to God for the answer, even when the only evidence you have of that answer is your own faith.

Another question often asked is: "When we repeat prayers more than once, aren't we praying 'vain repetitions'?"

Obviously, such people are referring to the admonition of Jesus when He told His disciples: **And when you pray do not (multiply words, repeating the same ones over and over, and) heap up phrases as the Gentiles do, for they think they will be heard for their much speaking** (Matt. 6:7 AMP). Praying the Word of God is not praying the kind of prayer that the "heathen" pray. You will note in 1 Kings 18:25-29 the manner of prayer that was offered to the gods who could not hear. That is not the way you and I pray. The words that we speak are not vain, but they are spirit and life, and mighty through God to the pulling down of strongholds. We have a God Whose eyes are over the righteous and Whose ears are open to us: when we pray, He hears us.

You are the righteousness of God in Christ Jesus, and your prayers will avail much. They will bring salvation to the sinner, deliverance to the oppressed, healing to the sick, and prosperity to the poor. They will usher in the next move of God in the earth. In addition to affecting outward circumstances and other people, your prayers will also have an effect upon you.

In the very process of praying, your life will be changed as you go from faith to faith and from glory to glory.

As a Christian, your first priority is to love the Lord your God with your entire being, and your neighbor as yourself. You are called to be an intercessor, a man or woman of prayer. You are to seek the face of the Lord as you inquire, listen, meditate and consider in the temple of the Lord.

As one of "God's set-apart ones," the will of the Lord for your life is the same as it is for the life of every other true believer: **...seek ye first the kingdom of God, and his righteousness; and all these things shall be added unto you** (Matt. 6:33).

# PERSONAL CONFESSIONS

Jesus is Lord over my spirit, my soul, and my body. (Phil. 2:9-11.)

Jesus has been made unto me wisdom, righteousness, sanctification, and redemption. I can do all things through Christ who strengthens me. (1 Cor. 1:30, Phil. 4:13.)

The Lord is my shepherd. I do not want. My God supplies all my need according to His riches in glory in Christ Jesus. (Ps. 23, Phil. 4:19.)

I do not fret or have anxiety about anything. I do not have a care. (Phil. 4:6, 1 Pet. 5:6,7.)

I am the Body of Christ. I am redeemed from the curse, because Jesus bore my sicknesses and carried my diseases in His own body. By His stripes I am healed. I forbid any sickness or disease to operate in my body. Every organ, every tissue of my body functions in the perfection in which God created it to function. I honor God and bring glory to Him in my body. (Gal. 3:13, Matt. 8:17, 1 Pet. 2:24, 1 Cor. 6:20.)

I have the mind of Christ and hold the thoughts, feelings, and purposes of His heart. (1 Cor. 2:16.)

I am a believer and not a doubter. I hold fast to my confession of faith. I decide to walk by faith and practice faith. My faith comes by hearing and hearing by the Word of God. Jesus is the author and the developer of my faith. (Heb. 4:14, Heb. 11:6, Rom. 10:17, Heb. 12:2.)

The love of God has been shed abroad in my heart by the Holy Spirit and His love abides in me richly. I keep myself in the Kingdom of light, in love, in the Word, and the wicked one touches me not. (Rom. 5:5, 1 John 4:16, 1 John 5:18.)

I tread upon serpents and scorpions and over all the power of the enemy. I take my shield of faith and quench his every fiery dart. Greater is He Who is in me than he who is in the world. (Ps. 91:13, Eph. 6:16, 1 John 4:4.)

I am delivered from this present evil world. I am seated with Christ in heavenly places. I reside in the Kingdom of God's dear Son. The law of the Spirit of life in Christ Jesus has made me free from the law of sin and death. (Gal. 1:4, Eph. 2:6, Col. 1:13, Rom. 8:2.)

I fear *not* for God has given me a spirit of power, of love, and of a sound mind. God is on my side. (2 Tim. 1:7, Rom. 8:31.)

I hear the voice of the Good Shepherd. I hear my Father's voice, and the voice of a stranger I will not follow. I roll my works upon the Lord. I commit and trust them wholly to Him. He will cause my thoughts to become agreeable to His will, and so shall my plans be established and succeed. (John 10:27, Prov. 16:3.)

I am a world overcomer because I am born of God. I represent the Father and Jesus well. I am a useful member in the Body of Christ. I am His workmanship recreated in Christ Jesus. My Father God is all the while effectually at work in me both to will and do His good pleasure. (1 John 5:4,5, Eph. 2:10, Phil. 2:13.)

I let the Word dwell in me richly. He who began a good work in me will continue until the day of Christ. (Col. 3:16, Phil. 1:6.)

# PRAYERS OF PRAISE

O magnify the Lord with me, and let us exalt His name together.

As for God, His way is perfect! The Word of the Lord is tested and tried; He is a shield to all those who take refuge and put their trust in him.

Let the words of my mouth and the meditation of my heart be acceptable in Your sight, O Lord, my firm, impenetrable rock and my redeemer.

Your Word has revived me and given me life.

Forever, O Lord, Your Word is settled in heaven.

Your Word is a lamp to my feet and a light to my path.

The sum of Your Word is truth and every one of Your righteous decrees endures forever.

I will worship toward Your Holy Temple, and praise Your name for Your loving-kindness and for Your truth and faithfulness; for You have exalted above all else Your name and Your Word, and You have magnified Your Word above all Your name!

Let my prayer be set forth as incense before You, the lifting up of my hands as the evening sacrifice. Set a guard, O Lord, before my mouth; keep watch at the door of my lips.

He who brings an offering of praise and thanksgiving honors and glorifies Me; and he who orders his way aright — who prepares the way that I may show him — to him I will demonstrate the salvation of God.

My mouth shall be filled with Your praise and with Your honor all the day.

Because Your loving-kindness is better than life, my lips shall praise You. So will I bless You while I live; I will lift up my hands in Your name.

Your testimonies also are my delight and my counselors.

## Scripture References (AMP)

| | |
|---|---|
| Psalm 34:3 | Psalm 138:2 |
| Psalm 18:30 | Psalm 142:2,3 |
| Psalm 19:14 | Psalm 50:23 |
| Psalm 119:50 | Psalm 71:8 |
| Psalm 119:89 | Psalm 63,3,4 |
| Psalm 119:105 | Psalm 119:24 |
| Psalm 119:160 | |

# PART I
# PERSONAL PRAYERS

# 1

# TO WALK IN THE WORD

Father, in the name of Jesus, *I commit myself to walk in the Word.* Your Word living in me produces Your life in this world. I recognize that Your Word is integrity itself — steadfast, sure, eternal — and I trust my life to its provisions.

You have sent your Word forth into my heart. I let it dwell in me richly in all wisdom. I meditate in it day and night so that I may diligently act on it. The Incorruptible Seed, the Living Word, the Word of Truth, is abiding in my spirit. That Seed is growing mightily in me now, producing Your nature, Your life. It is my counsel, my shield, my buckler, my powerful weapon in battle. The Word is a lamp to my feet and a light to my path. It makes my way plain before me. I do not stumble, for my steps are ordered in the Word.

The Holy Spirit leads and guides me into all the truth. He gives me understanding, discernment, and comprehension so that I am preserved from the snares of the evil one.

I delight myself in You and Your Word. Because of that, You put Your desires within my heart. I commit my way unto You, and You bring it to pass. I am confident that You are at work in me now both to will and to do all Your good pleasure.

I exalt Your Word, hold it in high esteem, and give it first place. *I make my schedule around Your Word.* I make the Word final authority to settle all questions that confront me. I choose to agree with the Word of God, and I choose to disagree with any thoughts, conditions, or circumstances contrary to Your Word. I boldly and confidently say that my heart is fixed and established on the solid foundation — the living Word of God!

## Scripture References

| | |
|---|---|
| Hebrews 4:12 | 1 Peter 3:12 |
| Colossians 3:16 | Colossians 4:2 |
| Joshua 1:8 | Ephesians 6:10 |
| 1 Peter 1:23 | Luke 18:1 |
| Psalm 91:4 | James 5:16 |
| Psalm 119:105 | Psalm 37:4,5 |
| Psalm 37:23 | Philippians 2:13 |
| Colossians 1:9 | 2 Corinthians 10:5 |
| John 16:13 | Psalm 112:7,8 |

# 2

# TO BE GOD-INSIDE MINDED

I am a spirit, I have a soul, and I live in a physical body. My spirit is the candle of the Lord. God, my Father, is guiding me into all the truth through my spirit.

I am a child of God, born of the Spirit of God, filled with the Spirit of God, and led by the Spirit of God. I listen to my heart as I look to my spirit inside me.

The Holy Spirit gives direction to my spirit and illumination to my mind. He leads me in the way I should go in all the affairs of life. He leads me by an inward witness. The eyes of my understanding are being enlightened. Wisdom is in my inward parts. His love is perfected in me. I have an unction from the Holy One.

I am becoming spirit-conscious. I listen to the voice of my spirit and obey what my spirit tells me. I let my spirit dominate me, for I walk not after the flesh, but after the spirit. I examine my leading in the light of His Word. I trust in the Lord with all my heart and lean not to my own understanding. In all my ways I acknowledge Him, and He directs my paths. I walk in the light of God's Word.

*I will educate and train and develop my human spirit.* The Word of God shall not depart out of my mouth. I meditate therein day and night. Therefore I shall make my way prosperous, and I will have good success in life. *I am a doer of the Word and put God's Word first.* My spirit man is in the ascendancy.

*Thanks be unto God who always causes me to triumph in Christ!*

## Scripture References

| | |
|---|---|
| 1 Thessalonians 5:23 | Job 38:36 |
| Proverbs 20:27 | 1 John 4:12 |
| John 16:13 | 1 John 2:20 |
| Romans 8:14,16 | Romans 9:1 |
| John 3:6,7 | Romans 8:1 |
| John 7:37-39 | Proverbs 3:5,6 |
| Ephesians 5:18 | Psalm 119:105 |
| Isaiah 48:17 | Joshua 1:8 |
| Ephesians 1:18 | James 1:22 |
| 1 Corinthians 1:30 | 2 Corinthians 2:14 |

# 3

# TO REJOICE IN THE LORD

Father, this is the day the Lord has made. I rejoice and I am glad in it! I rejoice in you always. And again I say, I rejoice. I delight myself in You, Lord. Happy am I because God is my Lord!

Father, You say that You rejoice over me with joy. Hallelujah! I am redeemed. I come with singing, and everlasting joy is upon my head. I obtain joy and gladness, and sorrow and sighing flee away. That spirit of rejoicing, joy, and laughter is my heritage. Where the Spirit of the Lord is there is liberty — emancipation from bondage, freedom. I walk in that liberty.

Father, my mouth shall praise You with joyful lips. I am ever filled and stimulated with the Holy Spirit. I speak out in psalms and hymns and make melody with all my heart to You, Lord. My happy heart is a good medicine and my cheerful mind works healing. The light in my eyes rejoices the heart of others. I have a good report. My countenance radiates the joy of the Lord.

Father, I thank You that I bear much prayer fruit. I ask in Jesus' name, and I will receive so that my joy (gladness, delight) may be full, complete, and overflowing. That joy of the Lord is my *strength*.

Therefore, I can count it all joy, all strength, when I encounter tests or trials of any sort because I am strong in You, Father.

I have the *victory* in the name of Jesus. Satan is under my feet. I am not moved by adverse circumstances. I have been made the righteousness of God in Christ Jesus. I dwell in the Kingdom of God and have peace and joy in the Holy Spirit! Praise the Lord!

## Scripture References

| | |
|---|---|
| Psalm 118:24 | Philippians 4:8 |
| Philippians 4:4 | Proverbs 15:13 |
| Philippians 3:1 | John 15:7,8 |
| Psalm 144:15 | John 16:23 |
| Zephaniah 3:17 | Nehemiah 8:10 |
| Isaiah 51:11 | James 1:2 |
| 2 Corinthians 3:17 | Ephesians 6:10 |
| James 1:25 | 1 John 5:4 |
| Psalm 63:5 | Ephesians 1:22 |
| Ephesians 5:18,19 | 2 Corinthians 5:7 |
| Proverbs 17:22 | 2 Corinthians 5:21 |
| Proverbs 15:30 | Romans 14:17 |

# 4

# TO WALK IN GOD'S WISDOM
# AND HIS PERFECT WILL

Father, I thank you that the communication of my faith becomes effectual by acknowledging every good thing which is in me in Christ Jesus. I hear the voice of the Good Shepherd. I hear my Father's voice, and the voice of a stranger I will not follow.

Father, I believe in my heart and say with my mouth that *this day the will of God is done in my life.* I walk in a manner worthy of You Lord, fully pleasing to You and desiring to please You in all things, bearing fruit in every good work. Jesus has been made unto me wisdom. I single-mindedly walk in that wisdom expecting to know what to do in every situation and to be on *top* of every circumstance!

I roll my works upon You, Lord, and You make my thoughts agreeable to Your will, and so my plans are established and succeed. You direct my steps and make them sure. I understand and firmly grasp what the will of the Lord is for I am not vague, thoughtless, or foolish. I stand firm and mature in spiritual growth, convinced and fully assured in everything willed by God.

Father, You have destined and appointed me to come progressively to know Your will — that is to perceive, to recognize more strongly and clearly, and to become better and more intimately acquainted with Your will. I thank you, Father, for the Holy Spirit who abides permanently in me and Who guides me into all the truth — the whole, full truth — and speaks whatever He hears from the Father and announces and declares to me the things that are to come. I have the mind of Christ and hold the thoughts, feelings, and purposes of His heart.

So, Father, I have entered into that blessed rest by adhering, trusting, and relying on You in the name of Jesus. Hallelujah!

### Scripture References

| | |
|---|---|
| Philemon 6 | Ephesians 5:17 |
| John 10:27 | Colossians 4:12 |
| John 10:5 | Acts 22:14 |
| Colossians 1:9,10 | 1 John 2:20,27 |
| 1 Corinthians 1:30 | 1 Corinthians 2:16 |
| James 1:5-8 | Hebrews 4:10 |
| Proverbs 16:3,9 | John 16:13 |

# 5

# TO WALK IN LOVE

Father, in Jesus' name, I thank You that the love of God has been poured forth into my heart by the Holy Spirit Who has been given to me. I keep and treasure Your Word. The love of and for You, Father, has been perfected and completed in me, and perfect love casts out all fear.

Father, I am Your child, and *I commit to walk in the God kind of love.* I endure long, am patient, and kind. I am never envious and never boil over with jealousy. I am not boastful or vainglorious, and I do not display myself haughtily. I am not rude and unmannerly and I do not act unbecomingly. I do not insist on my own rights or my own way for I am not self-seeking, touchy, fretful or resentful. I take no account of an evil done to me and pay no attention to a suffered wrong. I do not rejoice at injustice and unrighteousness, but I rejoice when right and truth prevail. I bear up under anything and everything that comes. I am ever ready to believe the *best* of others. My hopes are fadeless under all circumstances. I endure everything without weakening because my love never fails.

Father, I *bless* and *pray* for those who persecute me — who are cruel in their attitude toward me. I bless them and do not curse them. Therefore, my love abounds yet more and more in knowledge and in all judgment. I approve things that are excellent. I am sincere and *without offense* till the day of Christ. I am filled with the fruits of righteousness.

Everywhere I go I commit to plant seeds of love. I thank You, Father, for preparing hearts ahead of time to receive this love. I know that these seeds will produce Your love in the hearts to whom they are given.

Father, I thank You that as I flow in Your love and wisdom, people are being blessed by my life and ministry. Father, You make me to find favor, compassion, and loving) kindness with others (*name them*).

I am rooted deep in love and founded securely on love knowing that You are on my side, and nothing is able to separate me from Your love, Father, which is in Christ Jesus my Lord. Thank you, Father, in Jesus' precious name. Amen.

## Scripture References

| | |
|---|---|
| Romans 5:5 | Philippians 1:9-11 |
| 1 John 2:5 | John 13:34 |
| 1 John 4:18 | 1 Corinthians 3:6 |
| 1 Corinthians 13:4-8 | Daniel 1:9 |
| Romans 12:14 | Ephesians 3:17 |
| Matthew 5:44 | Romans 8:31,39 |

# 6

# TO WALK IN FORGIVENESS

Father, in the name of Jesus, I make a fresh commitment to You to live in peace and harmony, not only with the other brothers and sisters of the Body of Christ, but also with my friends, associates, neighbors, and family.

I let go of all bitterness, resentment, envying, strife, and unkindness in any form. I give no place to the devil in Jesus' name. Now Father, I ask Your forgiveness. By faith, I receive it, having assurance that I am cleansed from all unrighteousness through Jesus Christ. I ask You to forgive and release all who have wronged and hurt me. I forgive and release them. Deal with them in your mercy and loving-kindness.

From this moment on, I purpose to walk in love, to seek peace, to live in agreement, and to conduct myself toward others in a manner that is pleasing to You. I know that I have right standing with you and Your ears are attentive to my prayers.

It is written in Your Word that the love of God has been poured forth into my heart by the Holy Ghost Who is given to me. I believe that love flows forth into the lives of everyone I know, that I may be filled with and abound in the fruits of righteousness which bring glory and honor unto You, Lord, in Jesus' name. So be it!

## Scripture References

| | |
|---|---|
| Romans 12:16-18 | Mark 11:25 |
| Romans 12:10 | Ephesians 4:32 |
| Philippians 2:2 | 1 Peter 3:8,11,12 |
| Ephesians 4:31 | Colossians 1:10 |
| Ephesians 4:27 | Romans 5:51 |
| John 1:9 | Philippians 1:9,11 |

# 7

# TO WATCH WHAT YOU SAY

Father, today, I make a commitment to You in the name of Jesus. I turn from idle words and foolishly talking things that are contrary to my true desire to myself and toward others. Your Word says that the tongue defiles; that the tongue sets on fire the course of nature; that the tongue is set on fire of hell.

*In the name of Jesus, I am determined to take control of my tongue.* I am determined that hell will not set my tongue on fire. I renounce, reject, and repent of every word that has ever proceeded out of my mouth against You, God, and Your operation. I cancel its power and dedicate my mouth to speak excellent and right things. My mouth shall utter truth.

I am the righteousness of God. I set the course of my life for obedience, for abundance, for wisdom, for health, and for joy. Everything I speak is becoming to God. I refuse to compromise or err from pure and sound words. The words of my mouth and my deeds shall show forth Your righteousness and Your salvation all of my days. I guard my mouth and my heart with all diligence. I refuse to give Satan any place in me.

Father, Your Words are top priority to me. They are spirit and life. I let the Word dwell in me richly in all

43

wisdom. The ability of God is released within me by the words of my mouth and by the Word of God. I speak Your Words out of my mouth. They are alive in me. You are alive and working in me. So, I can boldly say that my words are words of faith, words of power, words of love, and words of life. They produce good things in my life and in the lives of others. Because I choose Your Words for my lips, I choose Your will for my life, and I go forth in the power of those words to perform them in Jesus' name.

## Scripture References

Ephesians 5:4

2 Timothy 2:16

James 3:6

Proverbs 8:6,7

2 Corinthians 5:21

Proverbs 4:23

Proverbs 21:23

Ephesians 4:27

James 1:6

John 6:63

Colossians 3:16

Philemon 6

# 8

# TO LIVE FREE FROM WORRY

Father, I thank You that I have been delivered from the power of darkness and translated into the Kingdom of Your dear Son. *I commit to live free from worry in the name of Jesus,* for the law of the Spirit of life in Christ Jesus has made me *free* from the law of sin and death.

I humble myself under Your mighty hand that in due time You may exalt me. I cast the whole of my cares (*name them*) — all my anxieties, all my worries, all my concerns, once and for all — on You. You care for me affectionately and care about me watchfully. You sustain me. You will never allow the consistently righteous to be moved — made to slip, fall, or fail!

Father, I delight myself in You, and You perfect that which concerns me.

I cast down imaginations (reasonings) and every high thing that exalts itself against the knowledge of You, and bring into captivity every thought to the obedience of Christ. I lay aside every weight and the sin of worry which does try so easily to beset me. I run with patience the race that is set before me, looking unto Jesus, the author and finisher of my faith.

I thank You, Father, that You are able to keep that which I have committed unto You. I think on (fix my mind on) those things that are true, honest, just, pure, lovely, of good report, virtuous, and deserving of praise. I let not my heart be troubled. I abide in Your Words, and Your Words abide in me. Therefore, Father, I do *not* forget what manner of person I am. I look into the perfect law of liberty and continue therein, being *not* a forgetful hearer, but a *doer of the Word* and thus blessed in my doing!

Thank You, Father. *I am carefree.* I walk in that peace which passes all understanding in Jesus' name!

## Scripture References

| | |
|---|---|
| Colossians 1:13 | Hebrews 12:1,2 |
| Romans 8:2 | 2 Timothy 1:12 |
| 1 Peter 5:6,7 | Philippians 4:8 |
| Psalm 55:22 | John 14:1 |
| Psalm 138:8 | James 1:22-25 |
| 2 Corinthians 10:5 | Philippians 4:6 |

# 9

# TO RECEIVE JESUS AS SAVIOR AND LORD

Father, it is written in Your Word that if I confess with my mouth that Jesus is Lord and believe in my heart that You have raised Him from the dead, I shall be saved. Therefore, Father, I confess that Jesus is my Lord. I make Him Lord of my life right now. I believe in my heart that You raised Jesus from the dead. I renounce my past life with Satan and close the door to any of his devices.

I thank You for forgiving me of all my sin. Jesus is my Lord, and I am a new creation. Old things have passed away. Now all things become new in Jesus' name. Amen.

## Scripture References

| | |
|---|---|
| John 3:16 | John 14:6 |
| John 6:37 | Romans 10:9,10 |
| John 10:10b | Romans 10:13 |
| Romans 3:23 | Ephesians 2:1-10 |
| 2 Corinthians 5:19 | 2 Corinthians 5:17 |
| John 16:8,9 | John 1:12 |
| Romans 5:8 | 2 Corinthians 5:21 |

# 10

# TO RECEIVE THE INFILLING OF THE HOLY SPIRIT

My heavenly Father, I am Your child, for I believe in my heart that Jesus has been raised from the dead, and I have confessed Him as my Lord.

Jesus said, "How much more shall your heavenly Father give the Holy Spirit to those who ask Him." I ask You now in the name of Jesus to fill me with the Holy Spirit. I step into the fullness and power that I desire in the name of Jesus. I confess that I am a Spirit-filled Christian. As I yield my vocal organs, I expect to speak in tongues for the Spirit gives me utterance in the name of Jesus. Praise the Lord!

### Scripture References

| | |
|---|---|
| John 14:16,17 | Acts 10:44-46 |
| Luke 11:13 | Acts 19:2,5,6 |
| Acts 1:8a | 1 Corinthians 14:2-15 |
| Acts 2:4 | 1 Corinthians 14:18,27 |
| Acts 2:32,33,39 | Ephesians 6:18 |
| Acts 8:12-17 | Jude 1:20 |

# 11

# BOLDNESS

Father, in the name of Jesus, I am of good courage, I pray that You grant to me that with all *boldness* I speak forth Your Word. I pray that freedom of utterance be given me that I may open my mouth to proclaim *boldly* the mystery of the good news of the Gospel — that I may declare it *boldly* as I ought to do.

Father, I believe I receive that *boldness* now in the name of Jesus. Therefore, I have *boldness* to enter into the Holy of Holies by the blood of Jesus. Because of my faith in Him, I dare to have the *boldness* (courage and confidence) of free access — an unreserved approach to You with freedom and without fear. I can draw fearlessly and confidently and *boldly* near to Your throne of grace and receive mercy and find grace to help in good time for my every need. I am *bold* to pray. I come to the throne of God with my petitions, and for others who do not know how to ascend to the throne.

I will be *bold* toward Satan, demons, evil spirits, sickness, disease, and poverty for Jesus is the Head of all rule and authority — of every angelic principality and power. Disarming those who were ranged against us, Jesus made a *bold* display and public example of

49

them triumphing over them. I am *bold* to say, "Satan, you are a defeated foe, for my God and my Jesus reign!"

I take comfort and am encouraged and confidently and *boldly* say, "The Lord is my Helper, I will not be seized with alarm — I will not fear or dread or be terrified. What can man do to me?" I dare to proclaim the Word toward heaven, toward hell, and toward earth. I am *bold* as a lion for I have been made the righteousness of God in Christ Jesus. I am complete in Him! Praise the name of Jesus!

## Scripture References

Psalm 27:14
Acts 4:29
Ephesians 6:19,20
Mark 11:23,24
Hebrews 10:19 AMP
Ephesians 3:12

Hebrews 4:16
Colossians 2:10,15
Hebrews 13:6
Proverbs 28:1
2 Corinthians 5:21

# 12

# HUSBANDS

Father, in the name of Jesus, I take Your Word and confess this day that I hearken to Your wisdom. My wife and I dwell securely in confident trust, and we are without fear or dread of evil. I make my ears attentive to skillful and godly wisdom, inclining and directing my heart and mind to understanding. I apply all of my power to the quest of wisdom and understanding.

I let not mercy, kindness, and truth forsake me. I bind them about my neck and write them on the tablet of my heart. I prize the wisdom of God highly and exalt her. She will exalt and promote me, bringing me honor because I embrace her. For You, Lord, are my confidence, firm and strong, and You keep my foot from being caught in a trap or hidden danger.

Where I go, the Word of God shall lead me. When I sleep, it shall keep me. When I awaken, it shall talk to me. Therefore, I will speak excellent and princely things, and the opening of my lips shall be for right things. All the words of my mouth are righteous — upright and in right standing with God — and there is nothing contrary to truth or crooked in them.

I live considerately with my wife, with an intelligent recognition of our marriage relationship. I honor my wife as physically the weaker. However, I realize that we are joint-heirs to the throne with Jesus spiritually. I do this in order that our prayers will not be hindered or cut off.

I confess that my wife and I are of one and the same mind, united in spirit, compassionate and courteous, tenderhearted and humbleminded. I believe for our welfare, happiness, and protection, because we love and respect each other.

Father, thank You that we are a couple of good report, that we are successful in everything we set our hands to. We are uncompromisingly righteous. We capture human lives for You as fishers of men. As we do this, we are confident that You are the Lord God Who teaches us to profit and leads us in the way we should go. We are abundantly supplied, with every need met, in the name of Jesus. We have obtained the favor of the Lord, and the will of God is done in our lives and in our children's lives.

## Scripture References

| | |
|---|---|
| Proverbs 1:33 | Proverbs 2:2 |
| Proverbs 3:3 | Proverbs 4:8 |
| Proverbs 3:26 | Proverbs 6:22 |
| Proverbs 8:6,8 | 1 Peter 3:7-9 |
| Proverbs 11:30 | Isaiah 48:17 |

# 13

# WIVES

Father, in the name of Jesus, I take Your Word and speak it out of my mouth and say that I have faith that I am a capable, intelligent, patient, and virtuous woman. I am far more precious than jewels. My value to my husband and family is far above rubies and pearls.

The heart of my husband trusts in me confidently and relies on and believes in me completely, so that he has no lack of honest gain or need of dishonest spoil.

Father, I will comfort, encourage, and do him only good as long as there is life within me. I gird myself with strength and spiritual, mental, and physical fitness for my God-given task. I taste and see that my gain from work with and for God is good. My lamp goes not out; it burns on continually through the night of any trouble, privation, or sorrow, and it warns away fear, doubt, and distrust.

I open my hand to the poor. I reach out my filled hands to the needy — whether in spirit, soul, or body. My husband is known as a success in everything he puts his hand to. Strength and dignity are my clothing, and my position in my household is strong. I am secure and at peace in knowing that my family is in readiness for the future.

I open my mouth with skillful and Godly wisdom, and in my tongue is the law of kindness and love. I look well to how things go in my household. The bread of idleness, gossip, discontent, and self-pity I will not eat.

My children rise up and call me blessed and happy. My husband boasts of and praises me, saying that I excel in all that I set my hand to. I am a woman who reverently and worshipfully loves You, Lord, and You shall give me the fruits of my hands. My works will praise me wherever I go, for Father, I confess that I am a submitted wife — simply because I want to be and I recognize Your authority. I thank You for my husband who is head over me, but who has given me (through the chain of command) the necessary power to do what Your Word says for me to do from Proverbs 31:10-31. I am as this woman is — a loving, successful, submitted wife — in the name of Jesus.

## Scripture References (AMP)

Proverbs 31:10-31

# 14

# HARMONIOUS MARRIAGE

Father, in the name of Jesus, it is written in Your Word that love is shed abroad in our hearts by the Holy Ghost Who is given to us. Because You are in us, we acknowledge that love reigns supreme. We believe that love is displayed in full expression enfolding and knitting us together in truth, making us perfect for every good work to do Your will, working in us that which is pleasing in Your sight.

We live and conduct ourselves and our marriage honorably and becomingly. We esteem it as precious, worthy, and of great price. *We commit ourselves to live in mutual harmony and accord with one another* delighting in each other, being of the same mind and united in spirit.

Father, we believe and say that we are gentle, compassionate, courteous, tender-hearted, and humble-minded. We seek peace, and it keeps our hearts in quietness and assurance. Because we follow after love and dwell in peace, our prayers are not hindered in any way, in the name of Jesus. We are heirs together of the grace of God.

Our marriage grows stronger day by day in the bond of unity because it is founded on Your Word and rooted and grounded in Your love. Father, we thank You for the performance of it, in Jesus' name.

## Scripture References

Romans 5:5

Philippians 1:9

Colossians 3:14

Colossians 1:10

Philippians 2:13

Philippians 2:2

Ephesians 4:32

Isaiah 32:17

Philippians 4:7

1 Peter 3:7

Ephesians 3:17,18

Jeremiah 1:12

# 15

# COMPATIBILITY IN MARRIAGE

Father, in the name of Jesus, I pray and confess that my spouse and I endure long and are patient and kind; that we are never envious and never boil over with jealousy. We are not boastful or vainglorious, and we do not display ourselves haughtily. We are not conceited or arrogant and inflated with pride. We are not rude and unmannerly, and we do not act unbecomingly. We do not insist on our own rights or our own way, for we are not self-seeking or touchy or fretful or resentful. We take no account of the evil done to us and pay no attention to a suffered wrong. We do not rejoice at injustice and unrighteousness, but we rejoice when right and truth prevail.

We bear up under anything and everything that comes. We are ever ready to believe the best of each other. Our hopes are fadeless under all circumstances. We endure everything without weakening. *Our love never fails* — it never fades out or becomes obsolete or comes to an end.

We are confessing that our lives and our family's lives lovingly express truth in all things that we speak truly, deal truly, and live truly. We are enfolded in love and have grown up in every way and in all things. We esteem and delight in one another, forgiving one another readily and freely as God in Christ has forgiven us. We are imitators of God and copy His example as well-beloved children imitate their father.

Thank You, Father, that our marriage grows stronger each day because it is founded on Your Word and on Your kind of love. We give You the praise for it all, Father, in the name of Jesus.

## Scripture References

| | |
|---|---|
| 1 Corinthians 13:4-8 AMP | Ephesians 4:15,32 |
| 1 Corinthians 14:1 | Ephesians 5:1,2 |

# 16

# THE CHILDREN

Father, in the name of Jesus, I pray and confess Your Word over my children and surround them with my faith — faith in Your Word that You watch over it to perform it! I confess and believe that my children are disciples of Christ taught of the Lord and obedient to Your will. Great is the peace and undisturbed composure of my children, because You, God, contend with that which contends with my children, and You give them safety and ease them.

Father, You will perfect that which concerns me. *I commit and cast the care of my children once and for all over on You, Father.* They are in Your hands, and I am positively persuaded that You are able to guard and keep that which I have committed to You. You are more than enough!

I confess that my children obey their parents in the Lord as His representatives, because this is just and right. My children _____ honor, esteem, and value as precious their parents; for this is the first commandment with a promise: that all may be well with my children and that they may live long on earth. I believe and confess that my children choose life and love You, Lord, obey Your voice, and cling to You; for

You are their life and the length of their days. Therefore, my children are the head and not the tail, and shall be above only and not beneath. They are blessed when they come in and when they go out.

I believe and confess that You give Your angels charge over my children to accompany and defend and preserve them in all their ways. You, Lord, are their refuge and fortress. You are their glory and the lifter of their heads.

As parents, we will not provoke, irritate, or fret our children. We will not be hard on them or harass them, or cause them to become discouraged, sullen, or morose, or feel inferior and frustrated. We will not break or wound their spirits, but we will rear them tenderly in the training, discipline, counsel, and admonition of the Lord. We will train them in the way they should go, and when they are old they will not depart from it.

O Lord, my Lord, how excellent (majestic and glorious) is Your name in all the earth! You have set Your glory on or above the heavens. Out of the mouth of babes and unweaned infants You have established strength because of Your foes, that You might silence the enemy and the avenger. I sing praise to Your name, O Most High. *The enemy is turned back from my children in the name of Jesus!* They increase in wisdom and in favor with God and man.

## Scripture References

| | |
|---|---|
| Jeremiah 1:12 | Psalm 91:11 |
| Isaiah 54:13 | Psalm 91:2 |
| Isaiah 49:25 | Psalm 3:3 |
| 1 Peter 5:7 | Colossians 3:21 |
| 2 Timothy 1:12 | Ephesians 6:4 |
| Ephesians 6:1-3 | Proverbs 22:6 |
| Deuteronomy 30:19,20 | Psalm 8:1,2 |
| Deuteronomy 28:13 | Psalm 9:2,3 |
| Deuteronomy 28:3,6 | Luke 2:52 |

# 17
# THE HOME

Father, I thank You that You have blessed me with all spiritual blessings in Christ Jesus.

Through skillful and godly wisdom is my house (my life, my home, my family) built, and by understanding it is established on a sound and good foundation. And by knowledge shall the chambers (of its every area) be filled with all precious and pleasant riches — great priceless treasure. The house of the uncompromisingly righteous shall stand. Prosperity and welfare are in my house in the name of Jesus.

My house is securely built. It is founded on a rock — revelation knowledge of Your Word, Father. Jesus is my Cornerstone. Jesus is Lord of my household. Jesus is our Lord — spirit, soul, and body.

Whatever may be our task, we work at it heartily as something done for You, Lord, and not for men. We love each other with the God kind of love, and we dwell in peace. My home is deposited into Your charge, entrusted to Your protection and care.

*Father, as for me and my house we shall serve the Lord in Jesus' name. Hallelujah!*

## Scripture References

Ephesians 1:3

Proverbs 24:3,4

Proverbs 15:6

Proverbs 12:7

Psalm 112:3

Luke 6:48

Acts 4:11

Acts 16:31

Philippians 2:10,11

Colossians 3:23

Colossians 3:14,15

Acts 20:32

Joshua 24:15

# 18

# PROSPERITY

Father, in the name of Your Son, Jesus, I confess Your Word over my finances this day. As I do this, I say it with my mouth and believe it in my heart and know that Your Word will not return to You void, but will accomplish what it says it will do.

Therefore, I believe in the name of Jesus that all my needs are met, according to Philippians 4:19. I believe that because I have given tithes and offerings to further your cause, Father, gifts will be given to me, good measure, pressed down, shaken together, and running over will they pour into my bosom. For with the measure I deal out, it will be measured back to me.

Father, You have delivered me out of the authority of darkness into the Kingdom of Your dear Son. Father, I have taken my place as your child. I thank You that You have assumed Your place as my Father and have made Your home with me. You are taking care of me and even now are enabling me to walk in love and in wisdom, and to walk in the fullness of fellowship with Your Son.

*Satan, I bind you from my finances, according to Matthew 18:18, and loose you from your assignment against me, in the name of Jesus.*

Father, I thank You that Your ministering spirits are now free to minister for me and bring in the necessary finances.

Father, I confess You are a very present help in trouble, and You are more than enough. I confess, God, You are able to make all grace — every favor and earthly blessing — come to me in abundance, so that I am always, and in all circumstances furnished in abundance for every good work and charitable donation.

## Scripture References

| | |
|---|---|
| Isaiah 55:11 | 2 Corinthians 6:16,18 |
| Philippians 4:19 | Matthew 18:18 |
| Luke 6:38 | Hebrews 1:14 |
| Mark 10:29,30 | 2 Corinthians 9:8 |
| Colossians 1:13 | Psalm 46:1 |

# 19

# DEDICATION FOR YOUR TITHES

I profess this day unto the Lord God that I have come into the inheritance which the Lord swore to give me. I am in the land which You have provided for me in Jesus Christ, the Kingdom of Almighty God. I was a sinner serving Satan; he was my god. But I called upon the name of Jesus, and You heard my cry and delivered me into the Kingdom of Your dear Son.

Jesus, as my Lord and High Priest, I bring the first fruits of my income to You and worship the Lord my God with it.

I rejoice in all the good which You have given to me and my household. I have hearkened to the voice of the Lord my God and have done according to all that He has commanded me. Now look down from your holy habitation from heaven and bless me as You said in Your Word. I thank You, Father, in Jesus' name.

## Scripture References

Deuteronomy 26:1,3,10,11,14,15    Colossians 1:13
Ephesians 2:1-5    Hebrews 3:1,7,8

# 20

# HEALTH AND HEALING

Father, in the name of Jesus, I confess Your Word concerning healing. As I do this, I believe and say that Your Word will not return to You void, but will accomplish what it says it will. Therefore, I believe in the name of Jesus that I am healed, according to 1 Peter 2:24. It is written in Your Word that Jesus himself took our infirmities and bore our sicknesses. Therefore, with great boldness and confidence I say on the authority of that written Word that I am redeemed from the curse of sickness, and I refuse to tolerate its symptoms.

*Satan, I speak to you in the name of Jesus and say that your principalities, powers, your spirits who rule the present darkness, and your spiritual wickedness in heavenly places are bound from operating against me in any way. I am the property of Almighty God, and I give you no place in me. I dwell in the secret place of the Most High God. I abide, remain stable and fixed under the shadow of the Almighty, whose power no foe can withstand.*

Now, Father, because I reverence and worship You, I have the assurance of Your Word that the angel of the Lord encamps around about me and delivers me from every evil work. No evil shall befall me, no plague or calamity shall come near my dwelling. I confess the

Word of God abides in me and delivers to me perfect soundness of mind and wholeness in body and spirit from the deepest parts of my nature in my immortal spirit even to the joints and marrow of my bones. That Word is medication and life to my flesh for the law of the Spirit of life operates in me and makes me free from the law of sin and death.

I have on the whole armor of God, and the shield of faith protects me from all the fiery darts of the wicked. Jesus is the High Priest of my confession, and I hold fast to my confession of faith in Your Word. I stand immovable and fixed in full assurance that I have health and healing now in the name of Jesus.

*Once this has been prayed, thank the Father that Satan is bound and continue to confess this healing and thank God for it.*

## Scripture References

| | |
|---|---|
| Isaiah 55:11 | Psalm 91:10 |
| 1 Peter 2:24 | Psalm 34:7 |
| Matthew 8:17 | 2 Timothy 1:7 |
| Galatians 3:13 | Hebrews 4:12,14 |
| James 4:7 | Proverbs 4:22 |
| Ephesians 6:12 | Romans 8:2 |
| 2 Corinthians 10:4 | Ephesians 6:11,16 |
| Psalm 91:1 | Psalm 112:7 |

# 21

# SAFETY

Father, in the name of Jesus, I thank You that You watch over Your Word to perform it. I thank You that I dwell in the secret place of the Most High and that I remain stable and fixed under the shadow of the Almighty whose power no foe can withstand.

Father, You are my refuge and my fortress. *No evil shall befall me — no accident shall overtake me — nor any plague or calamity come near my home.* You give Your angels special charge over me, to accompany and defend and preserve me in all my ways of obedience and service. They are encamped around about me.

Father, You are my confidence, firm and strong. You keep my foot from being caught in a trap or hidden danger. Father, You give me safety and ease me — *Jesus is my safety!*

*Traveling* — As I go, I say, "Let me pass over to the other side," and I have what I say. I walk on my way securely and in confident trust, for my heart and mind are firmly fixed and stayed on You, and I am kept in perfect peace.

*Sleeping* — Father, I sing for joy upon my bed because You sustain me. In peace I lie down and sleep, for You alone, Lord, make me dwell in safety. I lie down and I am not afraid. My sleep is sweet for You give blessings to me in sleep. Thank You, Father, in Jesus' name. Amen.

*Continue to feast and meditate upon all of Psalm 91 for yourself and your loved ones!*

## Scripture References

| | |
|---|---|
| Jeremiah 1:12 | Proverbs 3:23 |
| Psalm 91:1,2 | Psalm 112:7 |
| Psalm 91:10 | Isaiah 26:3 |
| Psalm 91:11 | Psalm 149:5 |
| Psalm 34:7 | Psalm 3:5 |
| Proverbs 3:26 | Psalm 4:8 |
| Isaiah 49:25 | Proverbs 3:24 |
| Mark 4:35 | Psalm 127:2 |
| Mark 11:23 | |

# 22

# VICTORY OVER FEAR

Father, in Jesus' name, I confess and believe that no weapon formed against me shall prosper, and any tongue that rises against me in judgment I shall show to be in the wrong. I believe I dwell in the secret place of the Most High. I shall remain stable and fixed under the shadow of the Almighty God whose power no foe can withstand — this secret place hides me from the strife of tongues.

I believe the wisdom of God's Word dwells in me, and because it does, I realize that I am without fear or dread of evil. In all my ways I know and acknowledge God and His Word; thus, He directs and makes straight and plain my pathway. As I attend to God's Word, it is health to my nerves and sinews, and marrow and moistening to my bones.

I am strengthened and reinforced with mighty power in my innerself by the Holy Spirit Himself Who dwells in me. God is my strength and my refuge, and I confidently trust in Him and in His Word. I am empowered through my union with Almighty God. This gives me the superhuman, supernatural strength to walk in divine health and to live in abundance.

God Himself has said, **I will never leave you without support or forsake you or let you down, my child. [I will] not, [I will] not, [I will] not in any degree leave you helpless or relax my hold on you ... assuredly not!** (Heb. 13:5 AMP)

I take comfort and am encouraged and confidently and boldly say, "The Lord is my helper. I will not be seized with alarm. I will not fear or be terrified, for what can man do to me?"

I confess and believe that my children are disciples taught of the Lord and obedient to God's will. Great is the peace and undisturbed composure of my children — because God Himself contends with that which contends with me and my children, and He gives them safety and eases them. God will perfect that which concerns me.

This Word of God that I have spoken is alive and full of power. It is active and operative. It energizes me, and it affects me. As I speak God's Word, it is sharper than any two-edged sword, and it is penetrating into my joints and into the marrow of my bones. It is healing to my flesh. It is prosperity for me. It is the magnificent Word of Almighty God. According to His Word that I have spoken, so be it! Hallelujah!

## Scripture References

Isaiah 54:17
Psalm 91:1
Psalm 31:20
Proverbs 3:6,8
Ephesians 3:16
Psalm 91:2

Ephesians 6:10
Hebrews 13:5,6 AMP
Isaiah 54:13
Isaiah 49:25
Psalm 138:8
Hebrews 4:12

# 23

# VICTORY OVER DEPRESSION

Father, You are my refuge and my high tower and my stronghold in times of trouble. I lean on and confidently put my trust in You, for You have not forsaken me. I seek You on the authority of Your Word and the right of my necessity. I praise You, the help of my countenance and my God.

Lord, You lift up those who are bowed down. Therefore, I am strong and my heart takes courage. I establish myself on righteousness — right standing in conformity with Your will and order. I am far even from the thought of oppression or destruction, for I fear not. I am far from terror, for it shall not come near me.

Father, You have thoughts and plans for my welfare and peace. *My mind is stayed on You,* for I stop allowing myself to be agitated and disturbed and intimidated and cowardly and unsettled.

*Satan, I resist you and every oppressive spirit in the name of Jesus. I resist fear, discouragement, self-pity, and depression. I speak the Word of truth, in the power of God, and I give you no place, Satan; I give no opportunity to you. I am delivered from oppression by the blood of the Lamb.*

Father, I thank You that I have been given a spirit of power and of love and of a calm and well-balanced mind. I have discipline and self-control. I have the mind of Christ and hold the thoughts, feelings, and purposes of His heart. I have a fresh mental and spiritual attitude, for I am constantly renewed in the spirit of my mind with Your Word, Father.

Therefore, I brace up and reinvigorate and cut through and make firm and straight paths for my feet — safe and upright and happy paths that go in the right direction. I arise from the depression and prostration in which circumstances have kept me. I rise to new life, I shine and am radiant with the glory of the Lord.

Thank You, Father, in Jesus' name that I am set free from every evil work. I praise You that the joy of the Lord is my strength and stronghold! Hallelujah!

### Scripture References

| | |
|---|---|
| Psalm 9:9,10 | Ephesians 4:27 |
| Psalm 42:5,11 | Luke 4:18,19 |
| Psalm 146:8 | 2 Timothy 1:7 |
| Psalm 31:22-24 | 1 Corinthians 2:16 |
| Isaiah 35:3,4 | Philippians 2:5 |
| Isaiah 54:14 | Ephesians 4:23,24 |
| Isaiah 50:10 | Hebrews 12:12,13 |
| Jeremiah 29:11-13 | Isaiah 60:1 |
| Isaiah 26:3 | Galatians 1:4 |
| John 14:27 | Nehemiah 8:10 |
| James 4:7 | |

# 24

# VICTORY OVER GLUTTONY

Father, it is written in Your Word that if I confess with my lips that Jesus is Lord and believe in my heart that You have raised Him from the dead, I shall be saved. Father, I am Your child and confess that Jesus Christ is Lord over my spirit, my soul, and my body. I make Him Lord over every situation in my life. Therefore, I can do all things through Christ Jesus who strengthens me.

Father, *I have made a quality decision to give You my appetite.* I choose *Jesus* rather than the indulgence of my flesh. I command my body to get in line with Your Word. I eat only as much as is sufficient for me. I eat and am satisfied.

When I sit down to eat, I consider what is before me. I am not given to the desire of dainties or deceitful foods.

Like a boxer, I buffet my body — handle it roughly, discipline it by hardships — and subdue it. I bring my body into subjection to my spirit man — the inward man — the real me. Not all things are helpful — good for me to do though permissible. I will not become the slave of anything or be brought under its power.

My body is for the Lord. I dedicate my body — presenting all my members and faculties — as a living sacrifice, holy and well pleasing to You, presenting them as implements of righteousness. I am united to You, Lord, and become one spirit with You. My body is the temple, the very sanctuary, of the Holy Spirit who lives within me, whom I have received as a gift from You, Father.

I am not my own. I was bought for a price, made Your own. So then, I honor You and bring glory to You in my body. Therefore, I always exercise and discipline myself, bringing under authority my carnal affections, bodily appetites, and worldly desires. I endeavor in all respects to have a clean conscience, void of offense toward You, Father, and toward men. I keep myself from idols — from anything and everything that would occupy the place in my heart due to You, from any sort of substitute for You that would take first place in my life.

I no longer spend the rest of my natural life living by my human appetites and desires, but I live for what You will! I am on my guard. I refuse to be overburdened and depressed, weighed down with the giddiness and headache and nausea of self-indulgence, drunkenness (on food), worldly worries and cares, for I have been given a spirit of power and of love and of a sound mind. I have discipline and self-control.

Father, I *do* resist temptation in the name of Jesus. I strip off and throw aside every encumbrance — unnecessary weight — and this gluttony which so readily tries to cling to and entangle me. I run with patient endurance and steady persistence the appointed course of the race that is set before me, looking away from all distractions to Jesus, the author and finisher of my faith.

Christ the Messiah *will* be magnified and get glory and praise in this body of mine and *will* be boldly exalted in my person. Thank You, Father, in Jesus' name! Hallelujah!

### Scripture References

| | |
|---|---|
| Romans 10:9,10 | Romans 6:13 |
| Philippians 4:13 | 1 Corinthians 9:27 |
| Deuteronomy 30:19 | 1 Corinthians 6:19,20 |
| Romans 13:14 | Romans 12:1 |
| Proverbs 25:16 | Luke 21:34 |
| 2 Timothy 1:7 | 1 Corinthians 6:12,13,17 |
| Proverbs 23:1-3 | James 4:7 |
| Hebrews 12:1,2 | Philippians 1:20 |

# 25

# IN COURT CASES

Father, in the name of Jesus, it is written in Your Word to call on You and You will answer me and show me great and mighty things. I put You in remembrance of Your Word and thank You that You watch over it to perform it.

I say that no weapon formed against me shall prosper and any tongue that rises against me in judgment I shall show to be in the wrong. This peace, security, and triumph over opposition is my inheritance as Your child. This is the righteousness which I obtain from You, Father, which You impart to me as my justification. I am far from even the thought of destruction, for I shall not fear and terror shall not come near me.

Father, You say You will establish me to the end — keep me steadfast, give me strength, and guarantee my vindication; that is, be my warrant against all accusation or indictment. Father, You contend with those who contend with me, and You perfect that which concerns me. I dwell in the secret place of the Most High, and this secret place hides me from the strife of tongues, for a false witness who breathes out lies is an abomination to You.

I am a true witness and all my words are upright and in right standing with You, Father. By my long forbearing and calmness of spirit the judge is persuaded, and my soft speech breaks down the most bonelike resistance. Therefore, I am not anxious beforehand how I shall reply in defense or what I am to say, for the Holy Spirit teaches me *in that very hour* and moment what I ought to say to those in the outside world. My speech is seasoned with salt.

I thank You, Father, that Satan and all menacing spirits are bound from operating against me, for I am strong in You, Lord, and in the power of Your might. Your shield of faith quenches every fiery dart. Thank You, Father, that I increase in wisdom and in stature and years, and in *favor* with You, God, and man. Praise the Lord!

## Scripture References

Jeremiah 33:3

Jeremiah 1:12

Isaiah 43:26

Isaiah 54:17

Isaiah 54:14

1 Corinthians 1:8

Isaiah 49:25

Psalm 138:8

Psalm 91:1

Psalm 31:20

Proverbs 6:19

Proverbs 14:25

Proverbs 8:8

Proverbs 25:15

Luke 12:11,12

Colossians 4:6

Matthew 18:18

Ephesians 6:10,16

Luke 2:52

# PART II
# INTERCESSORY PRAYERS
# FOR OTHERS

# 26

# THE BODY OF CHRIST

Father, we pray and confess Your Word over the Body of Christ. We pray that Your people be filled with the full, deep, and clear knowledge of Your Will in all spiritual things. We pray they live and conduct themselves in a manner worthy of You, Lord, fully pleasing to You and desiring to please You in all things, bearing fruit in every good work, and steadily growing and increasing in and by the knowledge of You, with fuller, deeper, and clearer insight.

We pray that the Body of Christ will be invigorated and strengthened with all power, according to the might of Your glory, to exercise every kind of endurance and patience with joy, giving thanks to You, Father, Who has qualified and made them fit to share the portion which is the inheritance of the saints (God's holy people) in the Light. You, Father, have delivered and drawn them to Yourself out of the control and the dominion of darkness and have transferred them into the Kingdom of the Son of Your love, in whom they have their redemption through His blood, which means the remission of their sins.

Father, You delight at the sight of the Body of Christ, standing shoulder to shoulder in such orderly array and the firmness and the solid front and steadfastness of their faith in Christ, leaning on Him in absolute trust and confidence in His power, wisdom, and goodness. They walk — regulate their lives and conduct themselves — in union with and conformity to Him, having the roots of their being firmly and deeply planted in Him, being continually built up in Him, becoming increasingly more confirmed and established in the faith.

Your people, Father, clothe themselves as Your own picked representatives — Your chosen ones, who are purified and holy and well-beloved by You — by putting on behavior marked by tender-hearted pity and mercy, kind feeling, gentle ways, and patience. They have the power to endure whatever comes, with good temper. They are gentle and forbearing with each other and, if they have a grievance or complaint against another, readily pardon each other. As You, Lord, have freely forgiven them, so do they also forgive.

Your people put on love and enfold themselves with the bond of perfectness — which binds everything together completely in ideal harmony. They let the peace from Jesus act as umpire continually in their hearts — deciding and settling with all finality all the questions that arise in their minds — in that peaceful state to which they are called. They are thankful, appreciative, giving praise to You always.

The Body of Christ lets the Word spoken by Christ the Messiah have its home in their hearts and minds. It dwells in them in all richness, as they teach, admonish, and train each other in all insight, intelligence, and wisdom in spiritual songs, making melody to You, Father, with Your grace in their hearts.

And whatever they do in word or deed, they do everything in the name of the Lord Jesus and in dependence upon His person, giving praise to You, Father, through Him!

## Scripture References

Colossians 1:9-14          Colossians 2:5-7
Colossians 3:12-17

# 27

# MINISTERS

Father, in the name of Jesus, we pray and confess that the Spirit of the Lord shall rest upon _____ . . .the spirit of wisdom and understanding, the spirit of counsel and might, the spirit of knowledge. We pray that as Your Spirit rests upon _____ He will make him/her of quick understanding because You, Lord, have anointed and qualified him/her to preach the Gospel to the meek, the poor, the wealthy, the afflicted. You have sent _____ to bind up and heal the brokenhearted, to proclaim liberty to the physical and spiritual captives, and the opening of the prison and of the eyes to those who are bound.

_____ shall be called the priest of the Lord. People will speak of him/her as a minister of God. He/she shall eat the wealth of the nations.

We pray and believe that no weapon that is formed against _____ shall prosper and that any tongue that rises against him/her in judgment shall be shown to be in the wrong. We pray that You prosper _____ abundantly, Lord — physically, spiritually, and financially.

We confess that _____ holds fast and follows the pattern of wholesome and sound teaching

in all faith and love which is for us in Christ Jesus.
_____ guards and keeps with the greatest love
the precious and excellently adapted Truth which has
been entrusted to him/her by the Holy Spirit who
makes His home in _____.

Lord, we pray and believe that, each and every day,
freedom of utterance is given _____, that he/she
will open his/her mouth boldly and courageously as
he/she ought to do to get the Gospel to the people.
Thank you, Lord, for the added strength which comes
superhumanly that You have given him/her.

We hereby confess that we shall stand behind
_____ and undergird him/her in prayer. We will
say only that good thing that will edify _____.
We will not allow ourselves to judge him/her, but will
continue to intercede for him/her and speak and pray
blessings upon him/her in the name of Jesus. Thank
You, Jesus, for the answers. Hallelujah!

### Scripture References

Isaiah 11:2,3      2 Timothy 1:13,14
Isaiah 61:1,6      Ephesians 6:19,20
Isaiah 54:17       1 Peter 3:12

# 28

# MISSIONARIES

Father, we lift before You those in the Body of Christ who are out in the field carrying the good news of the Gospel — not only in this country but also around the world. We lift those in the Body of Christ who are suffering persecution — those who are in prison for their beliefs. Father, we know that You watch over Your Word to perform it, that Your Word prospers in the thing for which You sent it. Therefore, we speak Your Word and establish Your covenant on this earth. We pray here and others receive the answer there by the Holy Spirit.

Thank You, Father, for revealing unto Your people the integrity of Your Word and that they must be firm in faith against the devil's onset, withstanding him. Father, You are their light, salvation, refuge, and stronghold. You hide them in Your shelter and set them high upon a rock. It is Your will that each one prospers, is in good health, and lives in victory. You set the prisoners free, feed the hungry, execute justice, rescue, and deliver.

*In Jesus' name, we bind you, Satan, and every menacing spirit that would stir up against God's people.*

We commission the ministering spirits to go forth and provide the necessary help for and assistance to these heirs of salvation. We and they are strong in the Lord and in the power of Your might, quenching every dart of the devil in Jesus' name.

Father, we use our faith covering these in the Body of Christ with Your Word. We say that no weapon formed against them shall prosper, and any tongue that rises against them in judgment they shall show to be in the wrong. This peace, security, and triumph over opposition is their inheritance as Your children. This is the righteousness which they obtain from You, Father, which You impart to them as their justification. They are far from even the thought of destruction, for they shall not fear and terror shall not come near them.

Father, You say You will establish them to the end — keep them steadfast, give them strength, and guarantee their vindication, that is, be their warrant against all accusation or indictment. They are not anxious beforehand how they shall reply in defense or what they are to say, for the Holy Spirit teaches them in that very hour and moment what they ought to say to those in the outside world, their speech being seasoned with salt.

We commit these our brothers and sisters in the Lord to You, Father, deposited into Your charge, entrusting them to Your protection and care, for You are faithful. You strengthen them and set them on a firm foundation and guard them from the evil one. We join our voices in praise unto You, Most High, and silence the enemy and avenger. Praise the Lord! Greater is He who is in us than he who is in the world!

## Scripture References

| | |
|---|---|
| Jeremiah 1:12 | Ephesians 6:10,16 |
| Isaiah 55:11 | Isaiah 54:14,17 |
| 1 Peter 5:9 | 1 Corinthians 1:8 |
| Psalm 27:1,5 | Luke 12:11,12 |
| 3 John 2 | Colossians 4:6 |
| 1 John 5:4,5 | Acts 20:32 |
| Psalm 146:7 | 2 Thessalonians 3:3 |
| Psalm 144:7 | Psalm 8:2 |
| Matthew 18:18 | 1 John 4:4 |
| Hebrews 1:14 | |

# 29
# PROSPERITY FOR MINISTERING SERVANTS

Father, how we praise You and thank You for Your Word, knowing that You watch over Your Word to perform it, and no Word of Yours returns void, but accomplishes that which You please, and it prospers in the thing for which You sent it.

Father, in the name of Jesus, we pray, confess and believe according to Your Word that those in Your Body who have sown the seed of spiritual good among the people reap from the people's material benefits, for You directed that those who publish the good news of the Gospel should live and get their maintenance by the Gospel.

We confess that Your ministers seek and are eager for the fruit which increases to the people's credit — the harvest of blessing that is accumulating to their account. The people's gifts are the fragrant odor of an offering and sacrifice which You, Father, welcome and in which You delight. You will liberally supply, fill to the full, the people's every need according to Your riches in glory in Christ Jesus.

We confess that those then who receive instruction in the Word of God share all good things with their teachers, contributing to their support. We confess that Your people will not lose heart and grow weary and faint in acting nobly and doing right, for in due time and at the appointed season they shall reap, if they do not loosen and relax their courage and faint.

So then, as occasion and opportunity are open to the people, they do good to all people not only being useful and profitable to them, but also doing what is for their spiritual good and advantage.

We confess that Your people are a blessing, especially to those of the household of faith — those who belong to God's family, the believers. Thus, we believe and confess Your people sow generously that blessings may come to someone. Your people then reap generously and with blessings, for You love, take pleasure in, prize above other things, and are unwilling to abandon or do without a cheerful, joyous, prompt-to-do-it giver whose heart is in his giving.

God, You are then able to make all grace, every favor and earthly blessing, come to Your people in abundance, so that they are always and under all circumstances possessing enough to require no aid or support and furnished in abundance for every good work and charitable donation.

As Your people give, their deeds of justice and goodness and kindness and benevolence go on and endure forever. And God, You provide the seed for the sower and bread for the eating, so you also will provide and multiply the people's resources for sowing and increase the fruits of their righteousness. Thus Your people are enriched in all things and in every way so that they can be generous, and their generosity, as it is administered by Your teachers, will bring thanksgiving to God.

As it is written, **Give and it shall be given unto you; good measure, pressed down, shaken together, and running over, shall men give into your bosom** (Luke 6:38). Praise the Lord!

### Scripture References

Jeremiah 1:12
Isaiah 55:11
1 Corinthians 9:11,14
Philippians 4:17-19

Galatians 6:6-10
2 Corinthians 9:6-11
Luke 6:38

# 30

# SUCCESS OF A MEETING

Father, in the name of Jesus, we openly confess that the Word of God will come forth boldly and accurately during the _____ (meeting) and that the people who hear Your Word will not be able to resist the wisdom and the inspiration of the Holy Spirit that will be spoken through Your minister(s) of the Gospel.

We confess that, as Your Word comes forth, an anointing of the Holy Spirit will cause people to open their spiritual eyes and ears and turn from darkness to light — from the power of Satan to You, God, and make Jesus their Lord.

We commit this meeting to You, Father, we deposit it into Your charge — entrusting this meeting, the people who will hear, and the people who will speak into Your protection and care. We commend this meeting to the Word — the commands and counsels and promises of Your unmerited favor. Father, we know Your Word will build up the people and cause them to realize that they are joint-heirs with Jesus.

We believe, Father, that as Your Word comes forth, an anointing will be upon the speaker and _____ (name) will be submitted completely to the Holy Spirit, for the Word of God that is spoken is alive and full of power, making it active, operative, energizing, and effective, being sharper than any two-edged sword. We believe that every need of every person will be met spiritually, physically, mentally, and financially.

We thank You, Father, and praise You that, because we have asked and agreed together, these petitions have come to pass. Let these words with which we have made supplication before the Lord be near to the Lord our God day and night, that He may maintain the cause and right of His people in the _____ (meeting) as each day of it requires! We believe that all the earth's people will know that the Lord is God and there is no other! Hallelujah!

## Scripture References

| | |
|---|---|
| James 5:16 | Acts 26:18 |
| Matthew 18:19 | Acts 20:32 |
| Ephesians 6:19 | Hebrews 4:12 |
| Acts 6:10 | Philippians 4:19 |
| Ephesians 1:18 | 1 Kings 8:59,60 |

# 31
# SALVATION OF THE LOST

Father, it is written in Your Word, **First of all, then
I admonish and urge that petitions, prayers,
intercessions and thanksgivings be offered on behalf
of all men** (1 Timothy 2:1 AMP).

Therefore, Father, we bring the lost of the world
this day — every man, woman, and child from here
to the farthest corner of the earth — before You. As we
intercede, we use our faith believing that thousands this
day have the opportunity to make Jesus their Lord.

*For everyone who has that opportunity, Satan, we bind
your blinding spirit of antichrist and loose you from your
assignment against those who have that opportunity to make
Jesus Lord.*

We ask the Lord of the harvest to thrust the perfect
laborers across these lives this day to share the good
news of the Gospel in a special way so that they will
listen and understand it. We believe that they will not
be able to resist the wooing of the Holy Spirit, for You,
Father, bring them to repentance by Your goodness and
love.

We confess that they shall see who have never been
told of Jesus. They shall understand who have never

heard of Jesus. And they shall come out of the snare of the devil who has held them captive. They shall open their eyes and turn from darkness to light — from the power of Satan to You, God!

## Scripture References

| | |
|---|---|
| 1 Timothy 2:1,2 AMP | Romans 2:4 |
| Job 22:30 | Romans 15:21 |
| Matthew 18:18 | 2 Timothy 2:26 |

# 32

# NATIONS AND CONTINENTS

Father, in the name of Jesus, we bring before You the nation (or continent) of _____ and its leaders. Father, You say in Your Word that you reprove leaders for our sakes so that we may live a quiet and peaceable life in all godliness and honesty.

We pray that skillful and godly wisdom has entered into the heart of _____ leaders and that knowledge is pleasant to them, that discretion watches over them and understanding keeps them and delivers them from the way of evil and from the evil men.

We pray that the upright shall dwell in the government(s)...that men and women of integrity, blameless and complete in Your sight, Father, shall remain, but the wicked shall be cut off and the treacherous shall be rooted out. We pray that those in authority winnow the wicked from among the good and bring the threshing wheel over them to separate the chaff from the grain, for loving-kindness and mercy, truth and faithfulness preserve those in authority and their offices are upheld by the people's loyalty.

We confess and believe that the decisions made by the leaders are divinely directed by You, Father, and their mouths should not transgress in judgment.

Therefore, the leaders are men and women of discernment, understanding, and knowledge so the stability of _____ will long continue. We pray that the uncompromisingly righteous be in authority in _____ so that the people there can rejoice.

Father, it is an abomination for leaders to commit wickedness. We pray that their offices be established and made secure by righteousness and that right and just lips are a delight to those in authority and that they love those who speak what is right.

We pray and believe that the good news of the Gospel is published in this land. We thank You for laborers of the harvest to publish Your Word that Jesus is Lord in _____. We thank You for raising up intercessors to pray for _____ in Jesus' name. Amen.

### Scripture References

| | |
|---|---|
| Psalm 105:14 | Proverbs 28:2 |
| Proverbs 2:10-15 | Proverbs 29:2 |
| Proverbs 2:21,22 | 1 Timothy 2:1,2 |
| Proverbs 20:26,28 | Acts 12:24 |
| Proverbs 21:1 | Psalm 68:11 |
| ·Proverbs 16:10,12,13 | |

\* \* \*

Here is a list of continents and nations to help you as you pray for the world:

## Continents:

| | |
|---|---|
| Africa | North America |
| Asia | Oceania |
| Europe | South America |

# Nations:

Afghanistan
Albania
Algeria
Andorra
Angola
Argentina
Ascension
Australia
Austria
Azores
Bahamas
Bahrain
Bangladesh
Barbados
Belgium
Belize
Benin
Bermuda
Bhutan
Bolivia
Botswana
Brazil
Brunei
Bulgaria
Burkina Faso
Burma
Burundi
Cameroon
Canada
Cape Verde
Cayman Islands

Central African
   Republic
Chad
Chile
China, People's
   Republic of
Colombia
Comoros
Congo
Corsica
Costa Rica
Cuba
Cyprus
Czechoslovakia
Denmark
Djibouti
Dominica
Dominican
   Republic
East Timor
Ecuador
Egypt
El Salvador
Equatorial Guinea
Estonia
Ethiopia
Faeroe Islands
Falkland Islands
Fiji
Finland
France
French Guiana

French Polynesia
Gabon
Gambia
German Democratic Republic (East Germany)
Germany, Federal Republic of (West Germany)
Ghana
Gibraltar
Great Britain
Greece
Greenland
Grenada
Guadeloupe
Guatemala
Guinea
Guinea-Bissau
Guyana
Haiti
Honduras
Hong Kong
Hungary
Iceland
India
Indonesia
Iran
Iraq
Ireland
Israel
Italy
Ivory Coast

Jamaica
Japan
Jordan
Kampuchea
Kenya
Kiribati
Korea, Democratic People's Republic (North)
Korea, Republic of (South)
Kuwait
Lao
Latvia
Lebanon
Leeward Islands
Lesotho
Liberia
Libya
Lithuania
Luxembourg
Macao
Madagascar
Madeira Islands
Malawi
Malaysia
Maldives
Mali
Malta
Martinique
Mauritania
Mauritius
Mexico

Monaco
Mongolia
Morocco
Mozambique
Nauru
Nepal
Netherlands
Netherlands
  Antiles
New Caledonia
New Zealand
Nicaragua
Niger
Nigeria
Norway
Oman
Pakistan
Panama
Papua New Guinea
Paraguay
Peru
Philippines
Pitcairn Islands
Poland
Portugal
Qatar
Reunion
Romania
Rwanda
St. Helena
St. Lucia
St. Pierre &
  Miquelon

St. Thomas &
  Principe
St. Vincent &
  The Grenadines
Santa Cruz Islands
Saudi Arabia
Senegal
Seychelles
Sierre Leona
Singapore
Solomon Islands
Somalia
South Africa
Spain
Sri Lanka
Sudan
Sunname
Swaziland
Sweden
Switzerland
Syria
Taiwan
Tanzania
Thailand
Togo
Tonga
Trinidad & Tobago
Tristan da Cunha
Tunisia
Turkey
Turks & Caicos
  Islands
Tuvalu (Ellice
  Islands)

Uganda
Union of Soviet
  Socialist
  Republics
  (Russia)
United Arab
  Emirates
United States of
  America
Uruguay
Vanuatu
Vatican City State

Venezuela
Vietnam
Western Samoa
Yemen Arab
  Republic
Yemen, People's
  Democratic
Republic of
  Yugoslavia
Zaire
Zambia
Zimbabwe

# 33

# PEACE OF JERUSALEM

Father, in the name of Jesus and according to your Word, I long and pray for the peace of Jerusalem, that its inhabitants may be born again. I pray that You, Lord, will be a refuge and a stronghold to the children of Israel. Father, Your Word says "multitudes, multitudes are in the valley of decision" and whoever calls upon Your name shall be delivered and saved. Have mercy upon Israel and be gracious to them, O Lord, and consider that they fight for their land to be restored. You, Lord, are their strength and stronghold in their day of trouble. We pray that they are righteous before You and that You will make even their enemies to be at peace with them. Your Word says You will deliver those for whom we intercede, who are not innocent, through the cleanness of our hands. May they realize that their defense and shield depends on You.

We thank You for Your Word, Lord, that You have a covenant with Israel and that You will take away their sin. They are Your beloved. Your Word also says that Your gifts are irrevocable, that You never withdraw them once they are given, and that You do not change your mind about those to whom You give Your grace or to whom You send Your call. Though they have been disobedient and rebellious toward You, Lord, we pray that now they will repent and obtain Your mercy and forgiveness through Your Son, Jesus. We praise You, Lord, for Your compassion and Your forgiveness to Your people. We praise You that they are under Your protection and divine guidance, that they are Your special possession, Your peculiar treasure, and that You will spare them, for we have read in Your Word that all Israel shall be saved!

Thank You, Father, for delivering us all from every evil work and the authority You have given us with the name of Jesus. We love You and praise You. Every day, with its new reasons, do we praise You!

Pray for the peace of Jerusalem! May they prosper that love you "the Holy City!" Peace be within your walls and prosperity within your palaces!

### Scripture References

| | |
|---|---|
| Joel 3:14 | Romans 11:29 |
| Job 22:30 AMP | Isaiah 45:17 |

# 34

# AMERICAN GOVERNMENT

Father, in Jesus' name, we give thanks for the United States and its government. We hold up in prayer before You the men and women who are in positions of authority. We pray and intercede for the president, the representatives, the senators, the judges of our land, the policemen, as well as the governors and mayors, and for all those who are in authority over us in any way. We pray that the Spirit of the Lord rests upon them.

We believe that skillful and godly wisdom has entered into the heart of our president and knowledge is pleasant to him. Discretion watches over him; understanding keeps him and delivers him from the way of evil and from evil men.

Father, we ask that You compass the president about with men and women who make their hearts and ears attentive to godly counsel and do that which is right in Your sight. We believe You cause them to be men and women of integrity who are obedient concerning us that we may lead a quiet and peaceable life in all godliness and honesty. We pray that the upright shall dwell in our government...that men and women blameless and complete in Your sight, Father, shall remain in these positions of authority; but the wicked shall be cut off our government and the treacherous shall be rooted out of it.

Your Word declares that **blessed is the nation whose God is the Lord** (Ps. 33:12). We receive Your blessing. Father, You are our refuge and stronghold in times of trouble (high cost, destitution, and desperation). So we declare with our mouths that Your people dwell safely in this land, and we *prosper* abundantly. We are more than conquerors through Christ Jesus!

It is written in Your Word that the heart of the king is in the hand of the Lord, and you turn it whichever way You desire. We believe the heart of our leader is in Your hand and that his decisions are divinely directed of the Lord.

We give thanks unto You that the good news of the gospel is published in our land. The Word of the Lord prevails and grows mightily in the hearts and lives of the people. We give thanks for this land and the leaders You have given to us, in Jesus' name.

*Jesus is Lord over the United States!*

### Scripture References

| | |
|---|---|
| 1 Timothy 2:1-3 | Deuteronomy 28:10,11 |
| Proverbs 2:10-12,21,22 | Romans 8:37 |
| Psalm 33:12 | Proverbs 21:1 |
| Psalm 9:9 | Acts 12:24 |

# 35
# SCHOOL SYSTEMS
# AND CHILDREN

Father, we thank You that the entrance of Your Word brings light and thank You that You watch over Your Word to perform it. Father, we bring before You the _____ school system(s) and the men and women who are in positions of authority within the school system(s).

We believe that skillful and godly wisdom has entered into their hearts; that Your knowledge is pleasant to them. Discretion watches over them; understanding keeps them and delivers them from the way of evil and from evil men. We pray that men and women of integrity, blameless, and complete in Your sight, remain in these positions, but that the wicked be cut off and the treacherous be rooted out in the name of Jesus. Father, we thank You for born-again, Spirit-filled people in these positions.

Father, we bring our children, our young people before You. We speak forth Your Word boldly and confidently, Father, that we and our households are saved in the name of Jesus. We are redeemed from the curse of the law for Jesus was made a curse for us. *Our sons and daughters are not given to another people.* We enjoy our children, and they shall not go into captivity, in the name of Jesus.

As parents, we train our children in the way they should go, and when they are old they shall not depart from it.

Our children shrink from whatever might offend You, Father, and discredit the name of Christ. They show themselves to be blameless, guileless, innocent, and uncontaminated children of God without blemish (faultless, unrebukable) in the midst of a crooked and wicked generation, holding out to it and offering to all the Word of Life. Thank You, Father, that You give them knowledge and skill in all learning and wisdom, and bring them into favor with those around them.

Father, we pray and intercede that these young people, their parents, and the leaders in the school system(s) separate themselves from contact with contaminating and corrupting influences. They cleanse themselves from everything that would contaminate and defile their spirits, souls, and bodies. We confess that they shun immorality and all sexual looseness — flee from impurity in thought, word or deed. They live and conduct themselves honorably and becomingly as in the open light of day. We confess and believe that they shun youthful lusts and flee from them in the name of Jesus.

*Satan, we speak to you in the name of Jesus. We bind you, the principalities, the powers, the rulers of the darkness, and wicked spirits in heavenly places and tear down strongholds using the mighty weapons God has provided for us in the name of Jesus. We bind up that blinding spirit of antichrist. We bind every spirit of the occult — astrology, witchcraft, every familiar spirit. We bind sexual immorality, idolatry, obscenity, and profanity. We bind those spirits of alcohol, nicotine, and drug addiction. We bind worldly wisdom in any form — every opposer to the truth. We bind every destructive, deceitful, thieving spirit. You are loosed from your assignment against _____ in the name of Jesus for they escape from the snare of the devil who has held them captive.*

We commission the ministering spirits to go forth and police the area dispelling the forces of darkness.

Father, we thank You that in Christ all the treasures of divine wisdom (of comprehensive insight into the ways and purposes of God) and all the riches of spiritual knowledge and enlightenment are stored up and lie hidden for us, and we walk in Him.

We praise You, Father, that we shall see _____ walking in the ways of piety and virtue, revering Your name, Father. Those who err in spirit will come to understanding and those who murmur discontentedly will accept instruction in the Way, Jesus, to Your will and carry out Your purposes in their lives, for You, Father, occupy first place in their hearts. We surround _____ with our faith.

Thank you, Father, that You are the delivering God. Thank You, that the good news of the Gospel is published throughout our school system(s). Thank You, for intercessors to stand on Your Word and for laborers of the harvest to preach Your Word in Jesus' name. Praise the Lord!

## Scripture References

Psalm 119:130
Jeremiah 1:12
Proverbs 2:10-12
Proverbs 2:21,22
Acts 16:31
Galatians 3:13
Deuteronomy 28:32,41
Proverbs 22:6
Philippians 2:15,16
Daniel 1:17
Daniel 1:9
1 John 2:17

2 Timothy 2:21
2 Corinthians 7:1
1 Corinthians 6:18
Romans 13:13
Ephesians 5:4
2 Timothy 2:22
Matthew 18:18
2 Timothy 2:26
Hebrews 1:14
Colossians 2:3
Isaiah 29:23,24

# 36

# SALVATION

Father, in the name of Jesus, we come before You in prayer and in faith, believing. It is written in Your Word that Jesus came to save the lost. You wish all men to be saved and to know Your Divine Truth, Therefore, Father, we bring _____ before You this day.

*Satan, we bind you in the name of Jesus and loose you from the activities in* _____*'s life!*

Father, we ask the Lord of the harvest to thrust the perfect laborer into his/her path, a laborer to share Your Gospel in a special way so that he/she will listen and understand it. As Your laborer ministers to him/her, we believe that he/she will come to his/her senses ...come out of the snare of the devil who has held him/her captive and make Jesus the Lord of his/her life.

Your Word says that You will deliver those for whom we intercede, who are not innocent, through the cleanness *of our hands*. We're standing on Your Word, and from this moment on, Father, we shall praise You and thank You for his/her salvation. We have committed this matter into Your hands and with our faith we see _____ saved, filled with Your Spirit, with a full and clear knowledge of Your Word. Amen — so be it!

*Each day after praying this prayer, thank the Lord for this person's salvation. Rejoice and praise God for the victory! Confess the above prayer as done! Thank Him for sending the laborer. Thank Him that Satan is bound. Hallelujah!*

## Scripture References

Luke 19:10
Matthew 18:18
Matthew 9:38

2 Timothy 2:26
Job 22:30

# 37

# SPIRIT-CONTROLLED LIFE

The law of the Spirit of life in Christ Jesus has made
_____ free from the law of sin and death.
His/her life is governed not by the standards and
according to the dictates of the flesh but controlled by
the Holy Spirit. _____ is not living the life of
the flesh. _____ is living the life of the Spirit.
The Holy Spirit of God dwells within, and directs and
controls him/her.

_____ is a conqueror and gains a
surpassing victory through Jesus who loved him/her.
_____ does not let himself/
herself be overcome by evil, but overcomes and masters
evil with good. _____ has on the full armor of
light. _____ clothes himself/herself with the
Lord Jesus Christ, the Messiah, and makes no provision
for indulging the flesh.

_____ is a doer of God's Word. He/she has
God's wisdom. He/she is peace-loving, courteous,
considerate, gentle, willing to yield to reason, full of
compassion and good fruits. _____ is free from
doubts, wavering, and insincerity. He/she is subject to
God.

_____ stands firm against the devil. _____ resists the devil and he flees from him/her. _____ comes close to God and God comes close to him/her. _____ does not fear for God never leaves him.

In Christ, _____ is filled with the Godhead: Father, Son, and Holy Spirit. Jesus is his/her Lord!

## Scripture References

Romans 8:2,4,9,14,31,37    James 3:17
Romans 12:21                      Hebrews 13:5
Romans 13:12,14                  James 4:7,8
James 1:22                          Colossians 2:10

# 38
# RENEW FELLOWSHIP

Father, You hasten Your Word to perform it. I believe and confess that _____ is a disciple of Christ, taught of You, Lord, and obedient to Your will. Great is his/her peace and undisturbed composure. _____ has You in person for his/her teacher. He/she has listened and learned from You and has come to Jesus.

_____ continues to hold to things he/she has learned and of which he/she is convinced. From childhood he/she has had knowledge of and been acquainted with the Word, which is able to instruct him/her and give him/her the understanding of the salvation which comes through faith in Christ Jesus. Father, You will heal _____, lead _____, and recompense _____, and restore comfort to _____.

Jesus gives _____ eternal life. He/she shall never lose it or perish throughout the ages, to all eternity. _____ shall never by any means be destroyed. You, Father, have given _____ to Jesus. You are greater and mightier than all else; no one is able to snatch _____ out of Your hand.

I pray and believe that _____ comes to his/her senses and escapes out of the snare of the devil who has held him/her captive; and that _____ would judge himself/herself.

*In the name of Jesus, Satan and every hindering spirit, you are bound in* _____*'s life.*

_____ has become a fellow-heir with Christ, the Messiah, and shares in all He has for him/her and holds the first newborn confidence and original assured expectation firm and unshaken to the end. _____ casts not away his/her confidence for it has great recompense of reward.

Thank You for giving _____ wisdom and revelation — quickening him/her to Your Word. Thank You that _____ enjoys fellowship with You and Jesus and with fellow believers.

## Scripture References

| | |
|---|---|
| Jeremiah 1:12 | 2 Timothy 2:26 |
| John 6:45 | 1 Corinthians 11:31 |
| Isaiah 54:13 | Matthew 18:18 |
| 2 Timothy 3:14,15 | Hebrews 3:14 |
| Isaiah 57:18 | Hebrews 10:35 |
| John 10:28,29 | Ephesians 1:17 |
| 1 John 5:16 | 1 John 1:3 |

# 39

# DELIVERANCE FROM SATAN AND HIS DEMONIC FORCES

*If the person for whom you are interceding has not confessed Jesus as Savior and Lord, pray specifically for his/her salvation if you have not already done so. Stand and thank the Father that it is done in the name of Jesus. Then pray:*

Father, in the name of Jesus, I come boldly to Your throne of grace and present _____ before You. I stand in the gap and intercede in behalf of _____ knowing that the Holy Spirit within me takes hold together with me against the evils that would attempt to hold _____ in bondage. I unwrap _____ from the bonds of wickedness with my prayers and take my shield of faith and quench every fiery dart of the adversary that would come against _____.

Father, You say that whatever I bind on earth is bound in heaven, and whatever I loose on earth is loosed in heaven. You say for me to cast out demons in the name of Jesus.

*So I speak to you, Satan, and to the principalities, the powers, the rulers of the darkness, and spiritual wickedness in high places and the demonic spirits of* _____

_____ (names of spirits) assigned to
_____. *I take authority over you and bind you away
from* _____ *in the mighty name of Jesus. You loose*
_____ *and let him/her go free in the name of Jesus. I
demand that you desist in your maneuvers now. Satan, you
are a spoiled and defeated foe.*

Ministering spirits of God, you go forth in the
name of Jesus and provide the necessary help to and
assistance for _____.

Father, I have laid hold of _____'s salvation
and his/her confession of the Lordship of Jesus Christ.
I speak of things that are not as though they were, for
I choose to look at the unseen — the eternal things of
God. I say that Satan shall not get an advantage over
_____: for I am not ignorant of Satan's devices.
I resist Satan and he has run in terror from
_____ in the name of Jesus. I give Satan no
place in _____. I plead the blood of the Lamb
over _____ for Satan and his cohorts are
overcome by that blood and Your Word. I thank You,
Father, that I tread on serpents and scorpions and over
all the power of the enemy in _____'s behalf.
_____ is delivered from this present evil world.
He/she is delivered from the powers of darkness and
translated into the Kingdom of Your dear Son!

Father, I ask You now to fill those vacant places
within _____ with Your redemption, Your Word,
Your Holy Spirit, Your love, Your wisdom, Your
righteousness, and Your revelation knowledge in the
name of Jesus.

I thank You, Father, that _____ is redeemed
by the blood of Jesus out of the hand of Satan. He/she

is justified and made righteous by the blood of Jesus and belongs to You — spirit, soul, and body. I thank You that every enslaving yoke is broken, for he/she will not become the slave of anything or be brought under its power in the name of Jesus. _____ has escaped the snare of the devil who has held him/her captive and henceforth does Your will, Father, which is to glorify You in his/her spirit, soul, and body.

Thank You, Father, that Jesus was manifested that He might destroy the works of the devil. Satan's works are destroyed in _____'s life in the name of Jesus. Hallelujah! _____ walks in the Kingdom of God which is righteousness, peace, and joy in the Holy Spirit! Praise the Lord!

*Once this prayer has been prayed, thank the Father that Satan and his cohorts are bound. Stand firm, fixed, immovable, and steadfast on your confessions of faith as you intercede on this person's behalf for* **greater is He that is in you, than he that is in the world** (1 John 4:4).

## Scripture References

| | |
|---|---|
| Hebrews 4:16 | 2 Corinthians 2:11 |
| Ezekiel 22:30 | James 4:7 |
| Romans 8:26 | Ephesians 4:27 |
| Isaiah 58:6 | Revelation 12:11 |
| Ephesians 6:16 | Luke 10:19 |
| Matthew 18:18 | Galatians 1:4 |
| Mark 16:17 | Colossians 1:13 |
| Ephesians 6:12 | Matthew 12:43-45 |
| Colossians 2:15 | 1 Corinthians 6:12 |
| Matthew 12:29 | 2 Timothy 2:26 |
| Hebrews 1:14 | 1 John 3:8 |
| Romans 4:17 | Romans 14:17 |
| 2 Corinthians 4:18 | |

# 40

# EMPLOYMENT

Father, in Jesus' name, we believe and confess Your Word over _____ today knowing that You watch over Your Word to perform it. Your Word prospers in _____ whereto it is sent! Father, You are his/her source of every consolation, comfort, and encouragement. _____ is courageous and grows in strength.

His/her desire is to owe no man anything but to love him. Therefore, _____ is strong and lets not his/her hands be weak or slack, for his/her work shall be rewarded. His/her wages are not counted as a favor or a gift, but as something owed to him. _____ makes it his/her ambition and definitely endeavors to live quietly and peacefully, minds his/her own affairs, and works with his/her hands. He/she is correct and honorable and commands the respect of the outside world, being self-supporting, dependent on nobody and having need of nothing, for You, Father, supply to the full his/her every need.

He/she works in quietness, earns his/her own food and other necessities. He/she is not weary of doing right and continues in welldoing without weakening. _____ learns to apply himself/herself to good deeds — to honest labor and honorable employment — so that he/she is able to meet necessary demands whenever the occasion may require.

Father, You know the record of his/her works and what he/she is doing. You have set before _____ a door wide open, which no one is able to shut.

_____ does not fear and is not dismayed, for You, Father, strengthen him/her. You, Father, help _____ in Jesus' name, for in Jesus _____ has perfect peace and confidence and is of good cheer, for Jesus overcame the world and deprived it of its power to harm _____. He/she does not fret or have anxiety about anything, for Your peace, Father, mounts guard over his/her heart and mind. _____ knows the secret of facing every situation, for he/she is self-sufficient in Christ's sufficiency. _____ guards his/her mouth and his/her tongue keeping himself/herself from trouble.

_____ prizes Your wisdom, Father, and acknowledges You. You direct, make straight and plain his/her path, and You promote him/her. Therefore, Father, _____ increases in Your wisdom (in broad and full understanding), and in stature and years, and in favor with You, Father, and with man!

## Scripture References

Jeremiah 1:12
Isaiah 55:11
2 Corinthians 1:3
1 Corinthians 16:13
Romans 13:8   -
2 Chronicles 15:7
Romans 4:4
1 Thessalonians 4:11,12
2 Thessalonians 3:12,13
Luke 2:52

Titus 3:14
Revelation 3:8
Isaiah 41:10
John 16:33
Philippians 4:6,7
Philippians 4:12,13
Proverbs 21:23
Proverbs 3:6
Proverbs 4:8

# 41
# FINDING FAVOR
# WITH OTHERS

Father, in the name of Jesus, You make Your face to shine upon and enlighten _____ and are gracious (kind, merciful, and giving favor) to him/her. _____ is the head and not the tail. _____ is above only and not beneath.

Thank you for favor for _____ who seeks Your Kingdom and Your righteousness and diligently seeks good. _____ is a blessing to You, Lord, and is a blessing to _____ (name them: family, neighbors, business associates, etc.). Grace (favor) is with _____ who loves the Lord Jesus in sincerity. _____ extends favor, honor, and love to _____ (names). _____ is flowing in Your Love, Father. You are pouring out upon _____ the spirit of favor. You crown him/her with glory and honor for he/she is Your child — Your workmanship.

_____ is a success today. _____ is someone very special with You, Lord. _____ is growing in the Lord — waxing strong in spirit. Father, You give _____ knowledge and skill in all learning and wisdom.

You bring _____ to find favor, compassion, and loving-kindness with _____ (names).

_____ obtains favor in the sight of all who look upon him/her this day in the name of Jesus. _____ is filled with Your fullness — rooted and grounded in love. You are doing exceeding abundantly above all that _____ asks or thinks for Your mighty power is taking over in _____.

Thank you, Father, that _____ is well-favored by You and by man in Jesus' name!

### Scripture References

| | |
|---|---|
| Numbers 6:25 | Psalm 8:5 |
| Deuteronomy 28:13 | Ephesians 2:10 |
| Matthew 6:33 | Luke 2:40 |
| Proverbs 11:27 | Daniel 1:17 |
| Ephesians 6:24 | Daniel 1:9 |
| Luke 6:38 | Esther 2:15,17 |
| Zachariah 12:10 | Ephesians 3:19,20 |

# 42

# IMPROVING COMMUNICATION

_____ is a disciple of Christ — taught of the Lord and obedient to His will. Great is his/her peace and undisturbed composure. _____ is constantly renewed in the spirit of his/her mind — having a fresh mental and spiritual attitude — and is putting on the new nature — the regenerate self — created in God's image, God-like in true righteousness and holiness.

His/her life lovingly expresses truth in all things — speaking truly, dealing truly, living truly. _____ is enfolded in love, growing up in every way and in all things into Him, who is the Head, even Christ, the Messiah, the Anointed One. His/her mouth shall utter truth. _____ speaks excellent and princely things — the opening of his/her lips is for right things. All the words of his/her mouth are righteous. There is nothing contrary to truth or crooked in them.

_____ inclines his/her heart to Your testimonies, Father, and not to covetousness (robbery, sensuality, or unworthy riches). _____ does not love or cherish the world. The love of the Father is in him. _____ is set free from the lust of the flesh (craving for sensual gratification), the lust of the eyes (greedy longings of the mind), and the pride of life (assurance in his own resources or in the stability of earthly things). _____ perceives and knows the truth and that nothing false is of the truth.

_____ prizes Your wisdom, Father, and exalts it, and it will exalt and promote him/her. _____ attends to God's Words; consents and submits to Your sayings. _____ keeps them in the center of his/her heart. For they are life to _____ and medicine to all his/her flesh. _____ keeps his/her heart with all diligence, for out of it flow the springs of life.

_____ will do nothing from factional motives through contentiousness, strife, selfishness, or for unworthy ends — or prompted by conceit and empty arrogance. Instead, in the true spirit of humility, _____ does regard others as better than himself/herself. _____ esteems and looks upon and is concerned for not merely his/her own interests, but also for the interests of others.

_____ lets this same attitude and purpose and humble mind be in him/her which was in Christ Jesus. Thank You, Father, in Jesus' name.

## Scripture References

| | |
|---|---|
| Isaiah 54:13 | Psalm 119:36 |
| Ephesians 4:23,24 | 1 John 2:15,16,21 |
| Ephesians 4:15 | Proverbs 4:8,20-23 |
| Proverbs 8:6-8 | Philippians 2:2 |

# 43

# PEACE IN A TROUBLED MARRIAGE

Father, in the name of Jesus, we bring _____ before You. We pray and confess Your Word over them, and as we do, we use our faith, believing that Your Word will come to pass.

Therefore we pray and confess that _____ will let all bitterness, indignation, wrath, passion, rage, bad temper, resentment, brawling, clamor, contention, slander, abuse, evil speaking, or blasphemous language be banished from them; also all malice, spite, ill will, or baseness of any kind. We pray that _____ have become useful and helpful and kind to each other, tenderhearted, compassionate, understanding, loving-hearted, forgiving one another readily and freely as You Father, in Christ, forgave them.

Therefore, _____ will be imitators of You, God. They will copy You and follow Your example as well-beloved children imitate their father. _____ will walk in love, esteeming and delighting in one another as Christ loved them and gave Himself up for them, a slain offering and sacrifice to You God, so that it became a sweet fragrance.

*Satan, we render you helpless in your activities in the lives of _____. We come against the spirit of separation and divorce, and we loose you from your assignment against them. Satan, your power is broken from their marriage in the name of Jesus.*

Father, we thank You that _____ will be constantly renewed in the spirit of their minds having a fresh mental and spiritual attitude. They have put on the new nature and are created in God's image in true righteousness and holiness. They have come to their senses and escaped out of the snare of the devil who has held them captive and henceforth will do Your will, which is that they love one another with the God kind of love, united in total peace and harmony and happiness.

Thank You for the answer, Lord. We know it is done now in the name of Jesus.

## Scripture References

| | |
|---|---|
| Ephesians 4:31,32 | Ephesians 4:23,24 |
| Ephesians 5:1,2 | 2 Timothy 2:26 |
| Matthew 18:18 | |

# 44

# SINGLE BELIEVER

_____ is united to the Lord and has become one spirit with Him. _____ shuns immorality and all sexual looseness. _____ flees from impurity in thought, word, or deed.

_____ will not sin against his/her body by committing sexual immorality. His/her body is the temple of the Holy Spirit, whom he/she has received as a gift from God. _____ is not his/her own. _____ was bought for a price and made God's own. _____ will honor God and bring glory to Him in his/her spirit, soul, and body which are God's.

_____ shuns youthful lusts and flees from them, and aims at and pursues righteousness — all that is virtuous and good, right living, conformity to the will of God in thought, word, and deed. He/she aims at and pursues faith, love, and peace — which is harmony and concord with others — in fellowship with all Christians, who call upon the name of the Lord out of a pure heart.

_____ shrinks from whatever might offend You, Father, or discredit the name of Christ. _____ shows himself/herself to be a blameless, guileless, innocent, and uncontaminated child of God

without blemish (faultless) in the midst of a crooked
and wicked generation, among whom _____ is
seen as a bright light shining out clearly in the dark
world, holding out to it and offering to all the Word
of Life. Thank You, Father, that Jesus is Lord.

## Scripture References

1 Corinthians 6:17-20    Philippians 2:12,15,16
2 Timothy 2:22

# 45

# SINGLE FEMALE
# TRUSTING GOD FOR A MATE

Father, in the name of Jesus, I believe that You are providing Your very best for _____. And the man who will be united with _____ in marriage has awakened to righteousness. Father, as You have rejoiced over Jerusalem, so shall the bridegroom rejoice over _____. Thank You, Father, that he will love _____ as Christ loves the Church. He will nourish, carefully protect, and cherish _____.

Father, I believe, because he is Your best, that doubts, wavering, and insincerity are not a part of him; but he speaks forth the oracles of God, acknowledging Your full counsel with all wisdom and knowledge. He does not speak or act contrary to the Word. He walks totally in love, esteeming and preferring others higher than himself.

Father, I believe that everything not of You shall be removed from _____'s life. And, I thank You for the perfecting of Your Word in her life that she may be thoroughly furnished unto all good works. Father, I praise You for the performance of Your Word in her behalf.

## Scripture References

| | |
|---|---|
| Isaiah 62:5 | James 3:17 |
| Ephesians 5:25 | Proverbs 8:8 |

# 46

# SINGLE MALE
# TRUSTING GOD FOR A MATE

Father, in the name of Jesus, I believe that You are providing a suitable helpmate for _____. Father, according to Your Word, one who will adapt herself to _____, respect, honor, prefer, and esteem him, stand firmly by his side, united in spirit and purpose, having the same love and being in full accord and of one harmonious mind and intention.

Father, You say in Your Word that a wise, understanding, and prudent wife is from You, and he who finds a true wife finds a good thing and obtains favor of You.

Father, I know that _____ has found favor in Your sight, and I praise You and thank You for Your Word, knowing that You watch over it to perform it.

## Scripture References

Ephesians 5:22,33          Proverbs 19:14
Proverbs 18:22             Philippians 2:2

# 47
# HEALING OF THE HANDICAPPED

Father, we come before you boldly and confidently knowing that You are not a man that You should lie and that You watch over Your Word to perform it. Therefore, Father, we bring before You those who are called handicapped and ill — mentally and physically. Father, by the authority of Your Word, we know without a doubt that it is Your will for these people — babies, children, and adults — to be made completely whole and restored in the name of Jesus.

We know, Father, that Satan, the god of this world, comes against Your handiwork. We know that You are the God of miracles, the God of love, power, and might. Through Your redemptive plan, what Jesus did on the cross and in the pit of hell for us, we, Your people, are redeemed from the curse of the law. The law of the Spirit of life in Christ Jesus has made us free from the law of sin and death. We are seated with Christ in heavenly places far above all satanic forces.

So we bring these people before Your throne of grace who have been attacked mercilessly mentally and physically — by Satan and his cohorts. We intercede in behalf of them and their families and loved ones.

*Satan, we speak to you and to the principalities, powers, rulers of the darkness of this world, and wicked spirits in heavenly places, and we bind you and loose them from your assignments against these people in the mighty name of the Lord Jesus. You can no longer harass or hinder these people who have the opportunity this day to make Jesus their Lord and Savior. We bind doubt, unbelief, fear, tradition, discouragement, depression, and oppression from operating against the parents, children, and individuals involved.*

Father, we pray for born-again, Spirit-filled people in positions of authority — administrators, teachers, doctors, nurses, orderlies, attendants, and volunteers. We pray that men and women of integrity, blameless and complete in Your sight, remain in these positions, but that the wicked be cut off and the treacherous be rooted out. Father, we pray for laborers of the harvest to go forth preaching the good news to the lost and to the Body of Christ.

We pray that You quicken these people to Your Word — that they be filled with wisdom and revelation knowledge concerning the integrity of Your Word, speaking faith-filled words and doing faith-filled actions. We pray for the infilling of the Holy Spirit, divine health, the fruit of the recreated human spirit, the gifts of the Holy Spirit, and deliverance. May they know that Jesus is their Source of every consolation, comfort, and encouragement and that they are to be sanctified spirit, soul, and body. We confess that they are redeemed from the curse of the law — redeemed from every sickness, disease, malady, affliction, defect, deficiency, deformity, injury, and every demon.

We speak healing to unborn infants in the wombs of mothers for **Lo, children are an heritage of the Lord and the fruit of the womb is his reward** (Ps. 127:3).

We speak restoration to damaged brain cells and activation of dormant brain cells. We speak normal intellect for one's age. We speak creative miracles to the parts of the body. We speak healing to all wounds. We speak words of life and say that they shall live in victory in this life and not die. We speak perfect soundness of mind and wholeness in body and spirit. We say that tongues are loosed and speech is distinct. We say ears hear and eyes see in the name of Jesus. We say demons are cast out bowing to the name of Jesus. We speak deliverance to bodies and minds, for You, Lord God, are the help of their countenance and the lifter of those bowed down — the joy of the Lord is their strength and stronghold!

We commission God's ministering spirits to go forth as they hearken to God's Word to provide the necessary help for and assistance to those we are praying for!

Father, no Word of Yours is void of the power that it takes to cause itself to come to pass! We establish Your Word on this earth, for it is already forever settled in heaven. Nothing is too hard or impossible for You. All things are possible to us who believe. We pray for more intercessors to stand with us. Let our prayers be set forth as incense before You — a sweet fragrance to You! Praise the Lord!

## Scripture References

Romans 3:4
Mark 11:23,24
Psalm 42:11
Acts 3:16
Matthew 8:17
Nehemiah 8:10
John 10:10
Proverbs 20:12
Matthew 9:37,38
Romans 8:2
Psalm 119:89
2 Corinthians 1:3
Matthew 18:18
Mark 9:23
Psalm 127:3

Mark 16:17
Jeremiah 1:12
1 Peter 2:24
Psalm 146:8
2 Corinthians 4:4
Mark 7:35
Psalm 103:20
Galatians 3:13
Luke 1:37
Ephesians 1:17,18
Ephesians 2:6
Jeremiah 32:27
1 Thessalonians 5:23
Proverbs 2:21,22
Psalm 141:2

# 48

# DELIVERANCE FROM CORRUPT COMPANIONS

*Satan, in Jesus' name, take your hands off
_____. I bind you from his/her life. You desist in
your maneuvers against him/her.*

Father, I thank You for delivering _____ from
corrupt and depraved people. I confess that _____
has awakened and returned to sober sense and his right
mind, and sins no more. _____ separates
himself/herself from contact with contaminating
influences and cleanses himself/herself from everything
that would defile his/her spirit, soul, and body.

_____ lives and conducts himself/
herself honorably and becomingly as in the open light
of day; not in reveling (carousing) and drunkenness,
not in immorality and debauchery (sensuality and
licentiousness), not in quarreling and jealousy.
_____ is done with every trace of wickedness
(depravity, malignity) and all deceit and insincerity
(pretense, hypocrisy, grudges, slander), and evil
speaking of every kind.

_____ is loyally subject (submissive) to the
governing (civil) authorities — not resisting nor setting

himself/herself up against them. _____ is obedient, prepared, and willing to do any upright and honorable work. _____ walks as a companion with wise men, and he/she shall be wise.

His/her sins have been forgiven. _____ is pardoned through the name of Jesus and because of confessing His name. _____ is victorious over the wicked one because he/she has come to know and recognize and be aware of the Father.

The Word dwells and remains in _____ and he/she dwells in the Son and in the Father always. God's nature abides in _____ — His principle of life remains permanently within _____ and he/she cannot practice sinning because he/she is born of God. The law of the Spirit of life in Christ Jesus has made _____ free from the law of sin and death. Thank You, Father, for watching over Your Word to perform it in Jesus' name!

## Scripture References

1 Corinthians 15:33,34a  Proverbs 28:7
2 Timothy 2:21  1 Thessalonians 5:22
2 Corinthians 7:1  1 John 2:12-16
Romans 13:13  1 John 2:21,24
1 Peter 2:1  1 John 3:9
Romans 13:1,2  Romans 8:2
Titus 3:1  Jeremiah 1:12
Proverbs 13:20

# 49

# DELIVERANCE FROM CULTS

Father, in the name of Jesus, we come before You in prayer and in faith believing that Your Word runs swiftly throughout the earth, for the Word of God is not chained or imprisoned. We bring before You _____ (those, and families of those, involved in cults).

Father, stretch forth Your hand from above, rescue and deliver _____ out of great waters, from the land of hostile aliens whose mouths speak deceit and whose right hands are right hands raised in taking fraudulent oaths. Their mouths must be stopped for they are mentally distressing and subverting _____ and whole families by teaching what they ought not teach, for the purpose of getting base advantage and disreputable gain. But praise God, they will not get very far for their rash folly will become obvious to everybody!

Execute justice, precious Father, for the oppressed. Set the prisoners free, open the eyes of the blind, lift up the bowed down, heal the brokenhearted, and bind up their wounds. Lift up the humble and down-trodden and cast the wicked down to the ground in the mighty name of Jesus.

Turn back the hearts of the disobedient, incredulous, and unpersuadable to the wisdom of the upright, and the knowledge of the will of God, in order to make ready for You, Lord, a people perfectly prepared in spirit, adjusted, disposed, and placed in the right moral state.

Father, You say in Your Word to refrain our voices from weeping and our eyes from tears, for our prayers shall be rewarded and _____ shall return from the enemy's land and come again to his/her own country. You will save our offspring from the land of their exile, from the east and the west — sons from afar and daughters from the ends of the earth. We shall see _____ walking in the ways of piety and virtue, revering Your name, Father. Those who err in spirit will come to understanding. Those who murmur discontentedly will accept instruction in the Way, Jesus. Father, You contend with those who contend with us, and You give safety to _____.

*Satan, we speak to you in the name of Jesus. We bind you, the principalities, the powers, the rulers of the darkness, and the wicked spirits in heavenly places, and we tear down strongholds using the mighty weapons God has provided for us in the name of Jesus. We speak to greed, selfishness, pride, arrogance, boastfulness, abuse, blasphemy, disobedience, ungratefulness, profanity, rebellion, perverseness, slander, immorality, ferocity, hatred, treachery, conceit, lust, materialism, error, deceit, spirit of antichrist, unworthiness, filthiness, cruelty, hostility, depravity, distortion, ungodliness, and falsity and loose you from all diabolical assignments against _____. We cancel all negative talking and doubt and unbelief. Satan, you will not use this against _____.*

We commission the ministering spirits to go forth and dispel these forces of darkness and bring _____ home in the name of Jesus.

Father, we believe and confess that _____ has had knowledge of and been acquainted with the Word which was able to instruct him/her and give him/her the understanding for salvation which comes through faith in Christ Jesus. Lord, we pray and believe that You certainly will deliver _____ and draw _____ to yourself from every assault of evil and preserve and bring _____ safe into Your heavenly Kingdom. Glory to You, Father, who delivers those for whom we intercede in Jesus' name!

*Once this prayer has been prayed for an individual, confess it as done. Thank the Father that he or she is delivered, returning from the enemy's land. Thank God that Satan is bound. Thank God for his/her salvation.*

## Scripture References

Psalm 147:15
2 Timothy 2:9
Psalm 144:7,8
Titus 1:11
2 Timothy 3:9
Psalm 146:7,8
Psalm 147:3-6
Luke 1:17
Jeremiah 31:16,17
Jeremiah 46:27

Isaiah 43:5,6
Isaiah 29:23,24
Isaiah 49:25
Matthew 18:18
2 Timothy 3:2-9
Hebrews 1:14
2 Timothy 3:15
2 Timothy 4:18
Job 22:30

# 50
# DELIVERANCE FROM HABITS

Father, in the name of Jesus and according to Your Word, I hereby believe in my heart and say with my mouth that Jesus is the Lord of _____'s life. I also confess that from this day forward _____ is set free and delivered from the habit(s) of _____ in the name of Jesus.

*Satan you and all your principalities, powers, and master spirits who rule the darkness, and spiritual wickedness in high places are bound up and _____ is loosed from you in the name of Jesus, as it is written in Matthew 18:18-19. No longer can you, Satan, harass or operate any of your unclean spirits or habits over _____. He/she will not become the slave of anything that exalts itself over the Word of God or be brought under its power.*

I hereby confess that _____ is strengthened and reinforced with mighty power in his/her innerself by the Holy Spirit who lives and dwells in his/her innermost being. _____ is strong in the Lord. He/she is empowered through his/her union with the Lord. He/she draws strength from the Lord — that strength which His boundless might provides.

_____ arms himself/herself with the full armor of God, that armor of a heavily armed soldier which God has supplied for him/her. . .the helmet of salvation. . .loins girded with truth. . .breastplate of righteousness. . .feet shod with the preparation of the gospel of peace. . .the shield of faith. . .and the Sword of the Spirit, which is the Word of God. With God's armor on, _____ is able to stand up against all the strategies and deceits and fiery darts of Satan in the name of Jesus.

As an act of his/her will and his/her faith, he/she receives complete and total freedom *now*. He/she is set free and delivered because he/she has called upon the name of the Lord, according to that which is written in His Word.

_____ is able to discipline his/her body and subdue it. He/she is strong. He/she is free. He/she withstands temptation, because Jesus is the Lord of his/her life. Jesus is his/her High Priest, and with Jesus and the Father on his/her side, _____ has the strength for all things. Greater is He that is in _____ than he that is in the world.

Thank You, Lord. I praise You that _____ is whole and redeemed from every evil work. With You and Your Word in _____, he/she controls his/her body. It does not nor can it ever again control him/her in the name of Jesus. Hallelujah!

### Scripture References

| | |
|---|---|
| Romans 10:9,10,13 | Hebrews 4:14-16 |
| Matthew 18:18,19 | 1 John 4:4 |
| 1 Corinthians 6:12 | Romans 8:4,9 |
| 2 Corinthians 10:4,5 | Romans 12:21 |
| Ephesians 3:16 | Romans 13:14 |
| Ephesians 6:10-17 | |

# ANSWERED PRAYERS

| Date | Explanation |
|------|-------------|
|      |             |
|      |             |
|      |             |
|      |             |
|      |             |
|      |             |
|      |             |
|      |             |
|      |             |
|      |             |
|      |             |
|      |             |
|      |             |
|      |             |
|      |             |
|      |             |
|      |             |

## ANSWERED PRAYERS

| Date | Explanation |
| --- | --- |
|  |  |
|  |  |
|  |  |
|  |  |
|  |  |
|  |  |
|  |  |
|  |  |
|  |  |
|  |  |
|  |  |
|  |  |
|  |  |
|  |  |
|  |  |
|  |  |
|  |  |
|  |  |
|  |  |

## ANSWERED PRAYERS

| Date | Explanation |
| --- | --- |
|  |  |
|  |  |
|  |  |
|  |  |
|  |  |
|  |  |
|  |  |
|  |  |
|  |  |
|  |  |
|  |  |
|  |  |
|  |  |
|  |  |
|  |  |
|  |  |
|  |  |
|  |  |
|  |  |
|  |  |
|  |  |

## ANSWERED
## PRAYERS

| Date | Explanation |
|------|-------------|
|      |             |
|      |             |
|      |             |
|      |             |
|      |             |
|      |             |
|      |             |
|      |             |
|      |             |
|      |             |
|      |             |
|      |             |
|      |             |
|      |             |
|      |             |
|      |             |
|      |             |
|      |             |
|      |             |

# ANSWERED PRAYERS

| Date | Explanation |
| --- | --- |
| | |
| | |
| | |
| | |
| | |
| | |
| | |
| | |
| | |
| | |
| | |
| | |
| | |
| | |
| | |
| | |
| | |
| | |
| | |

## ANSWERED
## PRAYERS

| Date | Explanation |
| --- | --- |
|  |  |
|  |  |
|  |  |
|  |  |
|  |  |
|  |  |
|  |  |
|  |  |
|  |  |
|  |  |
|  |  |
|  |  |
|  |  |
|  |  |
|  |  |
|  |  |
|  |  |
|  |  |

## ANSWERED
## PRAYERS

| Date | Explanation |
|------|-------------|
|      |             |
|      |             |
|      |             |
|      |             |
|      |             |
|      |             |
|      |             |
|      |             |
|      |             |
|      |             |
|      |             |
|      |             |
|      |             |
|      |             |
|      |             |
|      |             |
|      |             |
|      |             |

## ANSWERED PRAYERS

| Date | Explanation |
| --- | --- |
| | |
| | |
| | |
| | |
| | |
| | |
| | |
| | |
| | |
| | |
| | |
| | |
| | |
| | |
| | |
| | |
| | |
| | |
| | |
| | |

# ANSWERED PRAYERS

| Date | Explanation |
|------|-------------|
|      |             |
|      |             |
|      |             |
|      |             |
|      |             |
|      |             |
|      |             |
|      |             |
|      |             |
|      |             |
|      |             |
|      |             |
|      |             |
|      |             |
|      |             |
|      |             |
|      |             |

# ANSWERED PRAYERS

| Date | Explanation |
| --- | --- |
| | |
| | |
| | |
| | |
| | |
| | |
| | |
| | |
| | |
| | |
| | |
| | |
| | |
| | |
| | |
| | |
| | |
| | |
| | |
| | |
| | |

Ephesians 6-1

Children, obey your parents;
this is the right thing to do because
God has placed them in authority
over you.

# Books By
## Word Ministries, Inc.

*A Call To Prayer*

*Prayers That Avail Much — Volume I*

*Prayers That Avail Much — Volume II*

*Prayers That Avail Much — Special Edition*

*Prayers That Avail Much for Mothers*

*Prayers That Avail Much for Fathers*

*Prayers That Avail Much for Teens*

*The Prayers That Avail Much
Daily Planner and Prayer Diary*

Available from your local bookstore,
or by writing:

**HARRISON HOUSE**
P. O. Box 35035 • Tulsa, OK 74153

**Germaine Griffin Copeland** is Founder and President of Word Ministries, Inc. As the daughter of a Church of God minister, she knew in her early teens that God was calling her into the ministry. Only after she was married and had four children did Germaine realize her desperate need to know God personally. As she reached out to Him, He moved in and "old things passed away, and behold all things became new."

In 1969 Germaine began to grow in the knowledge of God's love and in the reality of overcoming faith. In 1972 God opened doors for her to share what she had learned. She began teaching with Women's Aglow Fellowship and within a few years became a renowned conference speaker. Later, Word Ministries, Inc. was formed and in 1980 published *Prayers That Avail Much*. Since that time, Germaine has shared her love of God with truth and in simplicity to many in congregations and in many seminars throughout the country. In 1984 she was called to the office of pastor of Word of Life Christian Fellowship in Smyrna, Georgia.

Today Germaine balances her home, the ministry and the pastoring of a flock with great wisdom and love. She ministers God's Word and the gifts of His Holy Spirit with tenderness and a deep desire to meet the needs of His people.

## The Harrison House Vision

Proclaiming the truth and the power
Of the Gospel of Jesus Christ
With excellence;

Challenging Christians to
Live victoriously,
Grow spiritually,
Know God intimately